# LANGUAGE AND LITERACY SERIES

Dorothy S. Strickland, FOUNDING EDITOR
Celia Genishi and Donna E. Alvermann, SERIES EDITORS
ADVISORY BOARD: Richard Allington, Kathryn Au, Bernice Cullinan, Colette Daiute,
Anne Haas Dyson, Carole Edelsky, Mary Juzwik, Susan Lytle, Django Paris, Timothy Shanahan

For volumes in the NCRLL Collection (edited by JoBeth Allen and Donna E.
(edited by Celia Genishi and Donna E. Alvermann), as well as other titles in

D0916623

# Personal Narrative, Revised

## Writing Love and Agency in the High School Classroom

**Bronwyn Clare LaMay**

Foreword by Andrea A. Lunsford

TEACHERS COLLEGE PRESS

**TEACHERS COLLEGE** | COLUMBIA UNIVERSITY
NEW YORK AND LONDON

NATIONAL WRITING PROJECT

Published simultaneously by Teachers College Press, 1234 Amsterdam Avenue, New York, NY 10027 and National Writing Project, 2105 Bancroft Way, Berkeley, CA 94720-1042.

Cover image by Owen LaMay

*Library of Congress Cataloging-in-Publication Data is available at loc.gov*

ISBN 978-0-8077-5808-3 (paper)
ISBN 978-0-8077-7515-8 (ebook)

Printed on acid-free paper
Manufactured in the United States of America

23  22  21  20  19  18  17  16      8  7  6  5  4  3  2  1

*To Diego, Hazel, Kylie, Serenity, Patrick, Nate, Alisha,
Sofia, Maizie, Abraham, and all of the students whose voices
and writings about love created this book.*

How can anyone be against love?
—Malcolm X

# Contents

# Foreword

*This is a book about love.* And about the role that love plays in the social, emotional, and academic lives of a group of students Bronwyn LaMay worked with for two years. As this ethnographic narrative makes strikingly clear, love turns out to have everything to do with how, why, and when these students engage—or not—with school and with the complex identities they are trying to build for themselves. While the students cannot define "love" precisely, they all know that it's there and that it's important, whether they embrace or reject its principles. As Hazel says, "The love's there, it might be hard to find, but it's one thing that can keep us together. One love." Reading about Hazel's journey, and the journeys taken by the other students in this book, has broadened my view of love. And it has changed, utterly, my understanding of how what Toni Morrison calls "generous love" can and must inform our teaching.

*This is a book about school gravity,* the push/pull that school factors exert in students' psyches. First defined by Diego, "school gravity" becomes a key concept for the class, as students seek to understand the forces that repel, but also sometimes attract, them to school. As Diego defines it, school gravity is all about relationships and the way school fosters or destroys relationships between students and school. Listen to the students in this book, and you will hear them speak eloquently about the disconnect they feel at school and about their understanding of what causes this disconnect. School gravity needs to be positive for students to learn and to prosper: As the students begin to rethink their relationship to school, they also begin to rethink their life stories—through writing.

*This is a book that is carefully theorized.* From Dewey and Freire and Burke and Bakhtin to Darling-Hammond, Elbow, Duncan-Andrade, Newkirk, Ladson-Billings, Shor, Nussbaum, Noguera, Rich, and a host of others, LaMay's argument is thoroughly informed by the best theories of how people learn and grow, both intellectually and emotionally.

*This is a book that connects school and personal life, writing and agency.* It would be a mistake to read *Writing Love and Agency* as grounded only in personal narrative or concerned only with personal stories. Rather, LaMay shows how deeply intertwined personal stories and academic writing can be. We meet Kylie, a student diagnosed with a learning disability and a quiet, unobtrusive presence in the class who didn't participate and who rarely did any of the work, especially writing. The "love narrative" got a response from her, however, and she wrote all the assignments, whether personal or academic. And as she wrote, Kylie's "personal and academic writing began to inform one another in ways that were representative of many students in the class," LaMay notes. The flexibility of the five core writing assignments, LaMay's steady but nondirectional guidance, and her intense and careful listening all helped students to connect to this "school writing" on their own terms in ways that allowed them to grow and, potentially, to change. As their personal narratives and their academic explorations of a literary text intertwined, their sense of agency grew.

*This is a book about Toni Morrison and her* Song of Solomon, to which the students referred, apparently without irony, as SOS. Still, many of these students were sending SOS signals of their own, and they recognized the extreme distress signals that run throughout Morrison's work. It may go without saying that choosing this novel was a gamble: At first, many students resisted; they would not read. But as LaMay began to read the book aloud, they came closer, and then closer. The characters and their life stories emerged as real, living people, people whose stories and counterplots in some cases matched those of students in the class. And then they read. They read this book with what I call a "fine-tooth eye," exploring, questioning, investigating, pushing to dig deeper into the narrative and to find both meaning and truth. They argued passionately about "Milkman moments" and about whether the characters had agency or were simply acted upon. They returned to scenes over and over, searching for deeper understanding. And most of all, they connected this book and its stories to their own lives. Together, they are a testament to the power of Morrison's imagination and to her concept of "generous love."

*This is a book about what really matters in school.* And what really matters is *courage* to know ourselves as teachers, with all our biases and flaws; *love* for ourselves as teacher/learners and love for our students as people as well as students; *openness and listening and respect* that open the doors for strong relationships; and *time* to commit to the effort.

Now turn the page and settle in to an enthralling account of writing, love, and agency.

Andrea A. Lunsford,
Louise Hewlett Nixon Professor of English Emerita,
Stanford University

*They ask me why I teach and I reply,*
*"Where could I find such splendid company?"*
*A Story (About a Teacher) Told By John Wooden*

## CHAPTER 1

# Defining School Gravity

**School Gravity:** *noun.* The magnetism (or alienation) that school factors create in a student's psyche, including, but not limited to, the class, the teacher, the substance of lessons, the teaching approach and expectations for learning, or any combination of pull factors, the central aspect being relational.

Definition Adapted from Diego Rosales, 11th Grade English

Around the second week in November, in my first semester of teaching what was then my 10th-grade class, I gave the following quiz one morning.

The Color of Water—Chapter 7 Quiz

Describe the race relations between Jews, Blacks, and Whites in Suffolk, Virginia.
Use at least two examples from Chapter 7.
You can talk about living conditions, life on the street, Tateh's views or things he would say, or anything else that is relevant. Just discuss the issue and show me that you've read.

Based on the pattern I had observed in the school year so far, I guessed that a handful of my students had read the assigned text and would be vaguely prepared to offer an informed response. The rest would try to write a circuitous, cursory answer, or turn in a blank quiz and admit they had not read the chapter.

I was watching my class when I noticed a student in the front corner busily writing, head bowed, pencil flowing, and wholly focused on the quiz in front of him. I was surprised, because this was not a student who usually read or turned in much homework. Diego Rosales was a visibly bright kid, but he had explained to me in the first week of school that his plan after graduation (if not before) was to join the Marines, following his older brother's path. Education was not something he found relevant to his life, and he had never had an experience with school that altered this view. This morning was the first time I had seen him engaged in my class, writing away, oblivious to distraction.

I momentarily jumped at the notion that maybe something in the novel had sparked him, that he might have heard or read something that had diverted his resistance. Maybe James McBride's text, which revolved around family relationships and racial identity in a context of bigotry, had hit a nerve. My mind raced to the possibilities for his excitement. Maybe my class had managed to prompt a flicker of interest in reading, maybe I could pull him in, maybe I could use his enthusiasm to help pull in other students. *Maybe ...*

Several minutes after most of the students were through writing, Diego handed me his quiz. My eyes scanned the page and saw that he had filled every line, including those on the back, with decorative handwriting that spilled out diagonally into the margins. After the class was over and I was in the room by myself, I sifted through the pile and pulled out his quiz in anticipation. His open response read as follows:

> I can't show you that I've read because I just haven't. Plus I don't lie, I try to be as honest as I can with people that I look up to. If I read the beginning of something and don't like it, I shut down. It's just how I am. I don't want to bull shit this quiz by pretending that I've read the story and try to answer the questions with "smart ass" answers. I look at everything and try to see how it can help me (now or in the future) and if it doesn't and I don't see a reason why I have to do it other than because someone told me to do it, I lose interest. Most of the time it's with reading, writing, and math. Not so much the writing part because my brother told me "you just have to write because all those things that go through your big ass head would be hard to remember if you don't put them down on paper." I like the book *Joker One*,[1] I'd like to thank you for going through the effort of getting me that book. Sorry I could be hard headed sometimes and just refuse to do some stuff sometimes.

I was momentarily disappointed. This was not the promising sign of budding intellectual awakening I had hoped for. Yet I appreciated Diego's honesty and his effort to articulate why my assignment felt irrelevant to him. Diego's feelings about reading or writing something that he did not connect to were common among my students. His wariness toward school and his casual disinterest were characteristic of many who consistently held back from *engaging* with academic content. I have worked with countless students who shared Diego's sentiment, but few expressed it so openly. Their skepticism surfaced in ways similar to the students Mike Rose describes in *Lives on the Boundary*, whose intuitive distrust of their education led them to "champion the average [and] rely on [their] own good sense" (1989, p. 29). By the time they were in high school, they had mastered a defense that could be tough to penetrate. Rose underscores the fact that many students "have to twist the knife in [their] own gray matter to make this defense work" (p. 29), a condition I have observed in the community where I taught—which I will name El Cuento—and in the school, which I will call Escenario High, where I was privileged to work with the same students for 2 consecutive years while I conducted my research as their English teacher.

## SCHOOL GRAVITY IN THE CONTEXT OF EL CUENTO

Alienation in school is the number one learning problem . . . when students want something badly, they move heaven and earth to get it.

—Ira Shor, *Pedagogy for Liberation: Dialogues on Transforming Education*

El Cuento is a city with a storied history of intergenerational gang conflict. It is also a city with a history characterized by fierce activism and collective struggle.

El Cuento proper is one of the 10 largest cities in America. Situated in a dense metropolitan area, it is similar to many cities in that it has a vast disparity in wealth. The affluent neighborhoods lie on the northern and western sides of the city in the heart of the technology industry. On the eastern side of downtown lie several barrios. Despite the recent economic meltdown, El Cuento continues to have one of the highest costs of living in the country, due mainly to the extremely high cost of housing. The annual median income in El Cuento's wealthiest areas is around $1.25 million, which contrasts starkly with a report from our principal that about 41% of our families live on an income of $14,000 per year or less.

Escenario High School was a small public charter school on El Cuento's east side with roughly 320 students across grades 9 through 12. The student population generally reflected the community it served: Approximately 80% of our students were Latino, and the rest consisted of a fairly even mix of African American, Pacific Islander, Vietnamese, and White youth. As a small school, we drew many students with special needs that were hard to address in the traditional large high school environment. One-third of the students in my class had an Individualized Education Program (IEP) and worked daily with our resource specialists, who supported full inclusion in almost all of their academic classes. Language was also an important consideration at our school, since half of our students were non-native English speakers, with one-quarter officially classified as English learners.

During the time that I served on the Escenario faculty, I was privileged to work with a competent and gifted group of educators who cared deeply about the day-to-day lives of our students. Many teachers on our staff showed genuine sensitivity to our students' individual needs and academic anxieties.

Since I shared my students with many teachers who were able to connect with them, their growth was a team effort. I collaborated with teachers across disciplines whose support for my research was key to getting it off the ground.

Our administration also granted us flexibility at the time to write curriculum as we saw fit, notwithstanding the constant pressure we faced as a school to raise our standardized test scores. Our school Annual Yearly Progress measure had grown over 200 points in the previous 2 years, but our annual standardized test scores were slightly lower than the local district schools. The second year I was at Escenario, when I collected the majority of my data, we were under intense pressure to raise test scores or face possible school closure. None of the educators at Escenario believed in standardized testing as a comprehensive measure of student growth and school success. We did not want it to be the soul of our school. However, our principal was clear with us at the beginning of the year that we would likely need to set these principles aside if we wanted to continue to exist.

It was clear to me that many of my students at Escenario held a remarkably one-dimensional view of school, mainly because they had experienced a one-dimensional education. Most of our students had spent their K–12 education in "underachieving" public schools during No Child Left Behind. Although these were the very students that NCLB mandated that we refuse to abandon, the obsessive testing that accompanied NCLB's policies over the previous decade had alienated many of these students from education. Debate over what a *quality* education meant for our students created a rift between our school and our charter network, which increasingly opted for a scripted, rote curriculum filled with standardized benchmarks, timed formulaic writing assessments, and instructional routines that asked students to demonstrate "knowledge" through multiple-choice exams. Linda Darling-Hammond describes this phenomenon in *The Flat World and Education*, noting that the "reduction of the curriculum to test prep happens most frequently and intensely in schools serving low-income and minority students where meeting test score targets is a greater struggle, leaving these students with the least access to the kind of learning that will prepare them for college and contemporary careers" (2010, p. 72). Like many other charter networks and districts under pressure to raise "achievement," our network moved toward a curriculum that was all assessment, all the time. The claim of many charter schools is to prepare all students for college, and ours was no exception. Yet the methods our network used in its concurrent drive for higher scores often compromised this mission, because its focus on test preparation often displaced college-preparatory curricula.

Test preparation practices also created a dynamic where we bombarded students with the promise that an education they found soulless and sometimes demeaning would lead to a more fulfilling life. It was a mixed message that discouraged trust. It was off-putting to students like Diego, who just didn't have enough positive experiences with education to see the point of it, and so developed the posture of "school's just not for me." His impulse to explain his thinking led him to articulate what he felt was wrong, and he experimented with writing out some of his views and sharing them with his teachers. In one example, he explained:

> I hate seeing students texting during class, listening to music, passing notes, talking over the teacher, and besides the common courtesy we lack at times, I understand why they do it—they don't know why they are there. So I want teachers who will debate and not hand referrals, teachers that will take time to educate and not take lunch to punish, to reason with students and not put down, and what's looking like the most important one today, teachers that will that will take their time teaching the life lessons that branch off of the subject they're teaching, not just jam in information so we could pass the next pointless fuckin test.

Many studies on engagement suggest that students are apt to disconnect from school when the culture prioritizes testing over intellectual inquiry and takes an impersonal approach to education (Connor & Pope, 2013; Newmann, 1992; Yazzie-Mintz, 2007). Ethan Yazzie-Mintz and Kim McCormick argue in one of these studies that a "focus on scores and outcomes, incentivized and dictated by state and federal policy, leaves many students feeling like . . . their value to the school community, particularly to the adults, is not based on who they are as developing adolescents, their potential for learning and growing, or their emerging passions and curiosity, but rather on their performance on standardized assessments" (2012, pp. 734–735). To Diego and many like him, school was suspect because it promoted an "education" that felt artificial through a rhetoric that spoke insincerely of equity, without taking students' real struggles into account. He argued that, to reach students like him, schools needed to go beyond *telling* students about the value of an education and instead provide an experience that actually felt valuable.

Diego invented the term *school gravity* to better convey his reasoning. The way I understood it, school gravity essentially meant that school could exert a pull on a student's psyche, depending on the class, the teacher, the substance of lessons, the teaching and learning environment, or any combination of these pull factors. Pull factors varied by student, and they were reasons why students chose to go to school. Conversely, these factors could be off-putting and become reasons why students chose to avoid school. Many scholars similarly define *engagement* as this matrix of authentic interconnection between students, teachers, the curricula, and the school community (Connor & Pope, 2013; Fredericks, Blumenfeld, & Paris, 2004). The basis of engagement is a mix of affective, behavioral, and intellectual buy-in, the central factor being *relational*.

Diego's definition of school gravity pointed to this idea that *engagement* with school necessitates a *relationship* with school. For many of my students, this relationship was fractured. The notion that it necessitates rebuilding is an aspect of school gravity that is distinct from other definitions of engagement. This is one reason why I adopt the term. Many of my students shared Diego's experiences and views to some extent, but they were not able to express their reasoning so clearly. At one point I asked my students to try to explain in writing the disconnect they felt from school and the reasons that could keep them from engaging with the work.

One student explained:

Some people just think that if they are in the hole already they can't get out and they are scared to try again because their mind is set that they are a failure. And they don't know how to change their mind.

Another student wrote:

At times I don't have that self-determination, which makes me not do the work. It's also partially because at times I feel like there is no use in doing some work that's not really going to help me for my future. And why should we be given a grade that labels our effort in school. It's honestly bull shit, and I can't really explain it to some teachers because they see it as an excuse. Even though I'm not trying to make excuses.

Someone raised a similar point from a different angle:

The disconnect is that we don't take into consideration the importance of finishing that essay on time or passing that exam, because we just don't see the importance of the essay as a life changing decision. When maybe in fact it might be in the long run.

And buried in the middle of Diego's paper, I found this line:

Why I think a lot of kids don't change is because I don't think you realize how big of a change you're asking.

Diego's point about the implication of asking for real change was accurate. There were many students in my class who were wary of what Hervé Varenne and Ray McDermott (1999) denote as the cultural currency of the classroom, who were open to learn and grow but were resistant to an ideology that promoted their comparison through grades, or blind faith in school as their social mobility tool. Many of my students were not inclined to appropriate a definition of achievement that tied their self-esteem to traditional markers of school success. They were, however, inclined to identify more with school when it connected them on a deeper level with meaningful, real-world problems that tied explicitly to their sense of self and their capacity for reflection and when it helped them nurture a sense of agency through connection to others.

In the last few years, some of my colleagues and I have explored the literature that speaks to two important ways in which students may form "academic identities" in relation to school and education. We have developed a theory that draws on two bodies of scholarship, which represent two distinct types of academic identity. We call these *instrumental academic identities* and *fundamental academic identities* (Wischnia, Nasir, LaMay, O'Connor, & Sullivan, 2010). We use the term *instrumental* to refer to a conception of school achievement that focuses on traditional measures such as grades and teacher evaluation and that holds a view of school as the primary path to life achievement. Scholars whose work focuses on instrumental academic identity look for ways in which students appropriate and internalize the traditional practices of school as valuable to their self-esteem (Steele, 1997) and relevant to present and future goals (Flores-Gonzales, 2002; Nasir, McLaughlin, & Jones, 2009).

The other line of research is more relevant to the perspectives my students express here and throughout the course of this book. This research focuses on what we call *fundamental academic identity* and explores students' relationships with school in light of their identities as *learners*, rather than their internalization of traditional achievement measures. Scholars within this paradigm focus on students' authentic participation in classroom communities that promote genuine disciplinary work, with implications for students' personal investment in their learning (Boaler & Greeno, 2000; Lee, 2007; Reveles & Brown, 2008). In this conception, students merge the work of self with the work of an academic discipline to form a relationship with school that becomes an integral part of how they see themselves.

Both lines of research describe connections between self and school that differ in critical ways, with implications for students like mine, who may not have equitable access to the positive school experiences that would enable them to be goal-oriented about education for its own sake, but who will—under the right circumstances—engage deeply in thinking and learning. I wanted my students to see the value in school, but I recognized that cramming in lectures about the value of grades and achievement was not the way to achieve this goal. Rather, I hoped to appeal to their identities as thinkers and learners by co-creating with them a curriculum that was relevant to their lives and offered them opportunities to develop the authentic, critical voice that is vital to engagement (Connor & Pope, 2013). At one point, Diego expressed to me, "I love education, I like feeling like I'm workin out my brain, I just hate the way school frames it and if you agree then what's stopping us from making our own frame the way we see fit?" Toward this end, my students and I aimed to define reading, writing, and revision as life processes with inherent potential for self-discovery and personal agency, through a curriculum that drew on our stories about love to intertwine socio-emotional and academic insight.

Two months after the school year ended, my principal called to tell me that my students' standardized test scores rose significantly during the spring of their junior year, which boosted our AYP out of the danger zone. There are several possible explanations for this. One is that more students took the test seriously and actually read the reading prompts. I do not think they were terribly concerned about the tests as 10th graders, when Diego's scores were the second lowest in my class. As juniors, they likely had more confidence and thought more carefully about the questions. They did not see value in the test, but they were more aware of the political context and chose to engage it in a more conscious way.

I do not suggest a direct correlation between the curricular approach I present in this book and my students' scores. I do suggest that in the current educational and political climate, educators can and should meet institutionally important outcomes most effectively by focusing on the humanity of the work.

## LOVE AND AGENCY IN OUR STORIES: SURVIVING "WHOLE"

Love can be hard to define. I pinpointed it as a topic that was real to my students' lives and that would hopefully become a door into the literature we would read in semester two of our second year. Love was possible to personalize as well as analyze in literary discussion, and it was a seminal theme in the novel I wanted them to read, which was Toni Morrison's *Song of Solomon*.

Love is salient to Morrison's writing because she identifies it as the crux of her work. In one her interviews, she explains, "actually, I think, all the time when I write, I'm writing about love or its absence . . . about love or how to survive—not to make a living, but how to survive *whole* in a world where all of us are, in some measure, *victims* of *something*" (Taylor-Guthrie, 1994, p. 40). This connection between love and surviving whole was relevant to my students, and it came out of our conversations that many of them struggled to process moments in their lives when they felt like victims of troubled relationships or life circumstances that were beyond their control. I noticed that they had trouble conveying these experiences without inadvertently writing themselves as victims in their larger life stories. This seemed to me a condition they shared with many of the novel's characters. Morrison maintains that "each one of us is in some way at some moment a victim and in no position to do anything about it . . . in a world like that, how does one remain whole—is it just impossible to do that?" (p. 40). Through a discussion that moved between Morrison's fiction and the complex, intimate concerns my students raised in our classroom community, we grew to realize that the answer to this question lay in a critical examination of the connection between love and agency in our own stories.

To scaffold the first day of reading, I asked my students to journal for about 10 minutes on the question, *What is love?* This writing session lasted much longer than I had planned. Two girls began to write and then stopped, on the verge of tears, asking if they could take a moment outside. A few students alternately wrote and stared vulnerably around the room. Several others were still writing determinedly when the 10 minutes were up and requested more time. On this and other journal topics, I always waited until almost everyone was finished and then asked if there were those who wanted to share. I also made it a point to journal each entry with my class and to share my writing with them if they wanted to hear it. This was the strategy that I used to scaffold and engage them in the first several chapters of the novel, as we journaled our way through topics that either they or I suggested could connect them to the reading. This initial topic of love, however, remained unsurpassed in the emotions that it raised. As students volunteered to read their work aloud, a spectrum of unresolved stories about relationships with parents, siblings, cousins, grandparents, boyfriends, and girlfriends—as well as conflicts within themselves—emerged and began to assume some perceptible patterns.

Our conversation lasted until the end of class. It felt unfinished, so as we delved into the novel's opening chapters, I asked them to push deeper to define love in the first personal narrative they would write.

A conceptual topic like love allowed students to choose how to respond and how personal to get. One student began with the dictionary and argued that love is hard to define, given the 11 different definitions that she found. Another wrote about how the media portrayed love in misleading ways. Some students wrote about the different loves they felt for family, friends, and significant others. Other students wrote about love as loss, love as fantasy, love as a fairy tale, love as rejection, love as security, and love as a push-pull roller coaster ride with volatile but predictable ups and downs. Several students wrote with conviction that love did not exist. Some wrote about feeling love-deprived. *All* of them struggled to various degrees to write these papers. As I read them, it grew apparent to me that many of their definitions of love were essentially metaphors for their outlooks on life.

In *The Dialogic Curriculum* (1995), Patricia Stock explores the issue of creating space in the classroom for students to raise and assess personal questions, especially those that connect to the literature they read. Many of my students struggled for perspective on problems in their lives that could take precedence over their focus in class. Stock addresses this point in her work, acknowledging:

> Some educators insist that teachers should not allow students to explore their personal concerns in the talk or writing they do in classrooms, even when students' concerns match those in the readings they are assigned. . . . I hold a position on this issue that I have not reached easily or lightly: Teachers of schoolchildren are never far from the concerns their students bring with them to their studies. If they are, they do not teach students. They may teach subject matter, but they do not teach students. (p. 76)

Her view was indispensable in the context where I taught. When my students were emotionally distressed, distracted, or withdrawn due to struggles in their personal lives, they were not able to engage personally or academically in class. This was an everyday reality that created stress for me and influenced my decision to invite them to raise real dilemmas in our classroom context. However, the relationships my students built with one another and with me over our first 18 months of working together were vital to the narrative approach I describe in this book, whereby we strove to study and respect our lives as texts.

## PERSONAL NARRATIVE: "PROCEDURES FOR LIFE-MAKING"

In *The Need for Story* (1994), Anne Haas Dyson and Celia Genishi describe youth as "narrated selves," or people who are essentially stories in progress. Their definition of narrative emerges from scholarship in narrative life study, conceptualized by Dan McAdams as "the narrative of the self—the personal myth—that I have tacitly, even unconsciously, composed over the course of my years. It is a story I continue to revise, and tell to myself (and sometimes to others) as I go on living" (1993, p. 11). The field of narrative life study develops from Jerome Bruner's elucidation of narrative knowing and builds on his premise that "a life as led is inseparable from a life as told" (2004, p. 36). He defines the personal narrative as a "set of procedures for 'life-making,'" whereby the purpose is to think critically about how we wring tellings from experience, given the alternative story choices we could make (2004, pp. 28–29). The power of recurrent stories to shape our future lies at the heart of the matter, as he explains, "in the end, we *become* the autobiographical narratives by which we 'tell about' our lives" (2004, p. 694).

This conceptualization differs from how narrative is typically taught in K–12 schools, but it is the type of narrative that I asked my students to write, revise, and weave into their academic analyses over the course of our work. As Thomas Newkirk (2014) notes in *Minds Made for Stories*, "in schools, narrative is often compartmentalized ('We do narrative in ninth grade'). Or we treat narrative as purely literary, removed from more practical purposes of persuading and informing" (p. 34). English curriculum does not typically present narrative as a genre that incorporates claims, evidence, reasoning, and other elements of argument. Rather, the Common Core State Standards highlight the teaching of narrative elements such as dialogue, description, characterization, and detail, and assess how a student creates and employs these. The standards do not inquire into how these literary elements embody students' identity development or internal dialogue or how they pose valuable opportunities for revision. It is as though the literary elements exist apart from students' lives. Narrative is traditionally perceived to follow a predictable plot pattern with rising and falling action, whereby conflict is often resolved. In life narratives, conflicts are frequently *not* resolved, and plotlines rise and fall in ways that offer opportunities for critical perception that is essential to our sense of agency. Newkirk contends:

> When we employ narrative—and approach experience as *caused* and comprehensible—we gain a measure of control. We take a stand against randomness and fatalism in favor of a world that makes sense. As creatures living in time, we rely on forms that help us understand our passage through time. If we accept this conception of narrative— as a foundational mode of understanding—we need to rethink the way we position it in our curriculum. (2014, p. 34)

Researchers in narrative life study perceive a connection between literary and life texts that support Newkirk's push to rethink its role in the academic curriculum and its relevance beyond the classroom. They argue that personal narratives engage traditional literary elements associated with English class in specific, unique ways (McAdams, 1993; Singer, 2005). For example, a *setting* is the background state of mind that we bring to our stories and real-time encounters. *Tone* reflects our internal voice and can indicate our outlook. *Characters* are those who grow to symbolize something beyond themselves in our lives. *Plot* is a narrative arc that is interpretive rather than objective and captures high and low points, turning points, and particularly vivid events and scenes. *Themes* can point to repeated feelings and experiences, or unresolved conflicts and desires. *Defenses* can leave stories without a sense of ambiguity or agency or with a me-against-the-world mentality that researcher Jefferson Singer (2001) names the *anti-story*.

All of these literary elements emerged in various combination in my students' work when they wrote about love. Chapter 2 explores how this substantive richness surfaced in excerpts from their love definitions.

Aspects of their identity work emerged in their papers as well. Scholars agree that we do more than tell a story when we narrate our lives—we construct fundamental pieces of our identity (McAdams, 1993; Newkirk, 1997). We convey elements of identity through stories and we grapple with identity decisions as we try to make them "tellable." As Robert Brooke (1987) explains, "When a writing teacher worries about her student's voice, she is also worrying about her student's identity" (1987, p. 149).

Narrative writing can be valuable for adolescents because it is inherent to the identity work that marks this developmental period. Researchers believe that adolescence marks the life story's ascent, as formal operational thinking prompts the tendency to question and contemplate our realities and personal truths (Erikson, 1968; Habermas & Bluck, 2000; McAdams, 1993; Piaget, 1968). As adolescents, we can start to understand the world in storied terms, and we craft stories—personal and collective—to convey who and how we are to others and ourselves. William Penuel and James Wertsch define identity along these lines as "a form of action that is first and foremost rhetorical, concerned with persuading others (and oneself) about who one is and what one values" (1995, p. 91). This rhetorical projection of self was evident in students' definitions of love, as they endeavored to write themselves as characters in their life stories.

Their definitions of love also revealed some of their most intimate ways of thinking. Morrison contends that the ways we love are the best reflection of who we are, because our truest selves emerge no matter how we try to veil them. She writes that "we love people pretty much the way we are . . . and in a way we are the way we love other people" (Taylor-Guthrie, 1994, p. 106). My students' love narratives, in many cases, embodied quintessential ways they conceptualized themselves and strove for agency in their lives.

Personal narratives can offer creative opportunity for analysis and inter-pretation, but they also have important implications for academic thinking and writing if we consider how genres intersect. This is a focus of Chapter 3. Many composition scholars propose that we can make academic discourse more relevant and accessible—in other words, lend it "school gravity"—by moving students between personal and academic writing and analysis (Elbow, 1995; Freire, 1987; Newkirk, 2014; Sullivan, 2003).

For many of my students, academic writing was off-putting. They consid-ered its conventions arbitrary and irrelevant, and they resented the idea that there was something substandard about the way they expressed themselves in informal writing or speech. Some were also unsure that they could succeed at academic writing, as one student, Sofia, explained, "I didn't really see myself doing the academics because I didn't really think I could do it." Many habitu-ally dismissed academic writing assignments, so I wanted to compel them to extend their personal writing to apply to literary essays in a way that could, in return, help them make sense of complex issues in their personal and social worlds. Composition scholars argue that "personal" and "academic" genres are not opposites; rather, they are hybrids that entwine in complementary ways (Elbow, 1991, 1995; Newkirk, 2014). Moreover, Newkirk (2014) argues that narrative embeds in the deep structure of all written genres. He claims that the positioning of academic argument is a form of narrative work, a notion that one of my students, Patrick, came to understand when he announced in class that "you grow academically off your past experiences."

To blend personal and literary analysis and to add complexity to the self-narrative, I introduced to my students the idea of a *narrative template*. This is a schematic structure, or a "cookie cutter plot," with potential to generate multiple stories in its likeness (Wertsch, 2008). It is a set story that we carry in our hearts and minds that holds creative power. It grew apparent to my students and myself that there were narrative templates underlying their definitions of love. This was how the idea of a *counterplot* came into our conversation. A counterplot is a fairly complex narrative construct that was evident in many of their bodies of work.

My students and I defined a counterplot as an internalized narrative template that acts like an undertow on our life trajectories. The term is from literary criticism. Geoffrey Hartman (1958) introduced it to explain the interrelationship of narratives in Milton's *Paradise Lost*. Hartman defined the counterplot as "a second plot, simultaneously expressed with the first," whose concealed presence is responsible for the narrative's counterpoint (p. 2). Contrary to what their names imply, plot and counterplot do not operate as two opposing or reverse narratives; instead, they create a kind of narrative incongruence. They tell two incompatible stories that are inextricable from each other, which contrast even as they parallel.

I brought this term into our class discussion because I felt that it applied to life narratives generally and that life narratives, like literary narratives, are *intertextual* (Kristeva, 1980). This means that they are made of multiple interwoven storylines that can coexist, collide, subsume, or counteract one another. This concept draws from Bakhtin's theory of dialogism, which proposes that "any text is the absorption and transformation of another" (1981, p. 66). In *Paradise Lost*, the intertextuality between plot and counterplot creates the intermittent effect of crisis followed by narrative stasis. It leads the narrative in a direction that feels cyclical but fixed.

This plot–counterplot dynamic ties to what Kenneth Burke (1953) terms *themes* or *patterns of experience*. Burke argues that experience is not purely a function of environment or of self but arises as a distinct interaction between the two. The ways that individuals adapt to adjust to specific environmental conditions may evolve into patterns of experience that come to distinguish them. As Burke explains, "arising presumably as a method of adjustment to one condition, the pattern may become a method of meeting other conditions—may become a typical manner of experiencing" (p. 152).

One student, Serenity, described a counterplot as "the things that force you to have a mentality already. Like what's in you and why you do things. And it's hard to see it in your own life because you really just see things as having to be like that." Diego also embedded this idea in his work, defining counterplot similarly as a story that gets *in* us when we don't know how it got there, to compel self-protective behaviors that paradoxically re-create the story we want to avoid. In one of his essays, he wrote, "It's hard to see the story underneath your own. Most would like to say there isn't one, that there's no deeper reason why they do what they do, other than the obvious. It took me a while to realize why I found myself in the same situation so many times. . . . There are so many stories buried underneath stories. Like a puppet master they manipulate us. It's often the things we do to prevent something from happening that let it happen."

Diego's determination to explicate his self-identified counterplot led to a question that became a theme in his writing: *Do we shape our stories or do our stories shape us?*

## STORYING THE ACADEMIC CURRICULUM

As a teacher-researcher, I was interested in how a curriculum built around these narrative concepts might help my students to develop an awareness of their personal narratives and interpreted patterns of experience. I was interested in how this awareness might be evidenced in the voice, perspectives, and content of their work and how it might influence their engagement and approach to literary analysis and essays. To my students, these questions translated simply to, *What is your story, and how is it serving you?*

To unpack this question, my students and I devised five assignments—three personal narratives and two essays—that built from one paper to the next. All three personal narrative topics and handouts were conceptualized and designed with student input. As students moved back and forth between personal and academic writing, I observed their evolving insights and revisions to their self-narratives as well as a rich interplay between genres as distinct narrative themes emerged and traversed their bodies of work. In many cases, their narrative work shaped their evolving interpretations of *Song of Solomon*, which in turn influenced their personal thinking about people and situations in their lives.

For example, Kylie, a student presented in Chapter 3, creatively combined her personal and academic thinking in a way that facilitated her development in both. She chose the complex personal problem of unhealthy personal relationships as a focus for her narrative work. Through her narratives, she was able to articulate and explore questions and dilemmas in her personal relationships in a way that offered an analytical frame for her initial reading of *Song of Solomon*, which developed into her first academic essay. Her analysis of Hagar and Milkman's relationship helped her identify problem spots in her personal narrative and consider possible reframings of how she was "writing" herself—not just in relationships but in life. Her third personal narrative became an important point of revision for her. She tried to adjust her former interpretation of her unhealthy relationship, which carried into her final essay and led to a more complex analysis of Hagar and Milkman and the chemistry between them.

As I read my students' work, my methods of analysis followed my methods of teaching. I listened for their affective setting, tone, and voice, and I looked for characters who appeared in multiple papers and played symbolic roles in their lives. I looked for passive and active grammatical constructions and for moments when students pointed to sources of agency that were external or internal to themselves. I looked for emerging patterns in their interpretations of life and literary events and for narrative themes that developed and stretched across their bodies of work. I looked for intertextualities among their papers, interviews, and reflections as they extended their thinking over the course of the five assignments. Essentially, I looked for ways that students emerged in their writing on *my* terms, then created their own language and themes and metaphors, and moved their understandings to *their* terms.

The students I discuss in this book generally represent the level and depth of work in the class, although different students peaked at various moments and engaged with the curriculum in different ways. Some participated brilliantly in class but did not apply themselves to the written work despite my pleading and prodding. Others listened attentively, spoke rarely, and tackled every written assignment. Two students chose to substitute academic essays for the personal narratives, an option that was open to all students if they felt uncomfortable with the narrative work. Two students who had routinely avoided my writing assignments wrote lengthy responses to all three of the personal narratives and declined to write the academic papers. Two others doubted my approach and were never on board with any of it. They told me in their reflections that they did not connect with the theme of love and felt the reading and subsequent writing assignments were "too personal." Meanwhile, one student wrote sob stories over and over, and one senior who was not enrolled in my class began coming daily and participating in our reading and class discussion, despite the fact that he was not receiving course credit.

Out of this mix emerged several students who engaged in courageous and compelling writing and revision. A focus of Chapters 4, 5, and 6 is to stretch a traditional view of revision, to show how the process can occur over multiple pieces and run concurrently along academic and personal lines. To lend school gravity to the idea of revision, I pushed my students to think of it as a living process with transformational undertones—not as the seemingly sterile act of fixing grammatical errors, but as a more compelling, intimate process of reframing the stories we live by. In this, I drew from Adrienne Rich, who defines revision as "looking back . . . seeing with fresh eyes . . . entering an old text from a critical direction" (1979, p. 35). I also looked to Paulo Freire's description of revision as a form of praxis, whereby we can increase our perceptual capacity and engage with our world in a "certain form of *writing* it or *rewriting* it, that is, of transforming it by means of conscious, practical work" (1987, p. 10).

Several of my students' narrative and essay revisions exemplify what Shor (1987) calls *situated pedagogy*. As they wrote their way through multiple papers, some of them learned to resituate their personal narratives within broader socio-historical narratives that helped to re-contextualize their meaning. Shor identifies the tendency for students who are "unaware of the connections between their own lives and society [to] personalize their problems" (p. 89). A purpose of our narrative work, then, was not to personalize problems, but to *depersonalize* them. This necessitated a shift from a personal frame to a larger scope to help students perceive how social inequities or abuses could play out in individual lives.

Bruce Perry and Maia Szalavitz, authors of *The Boy Who Was Raised as a Dog* (2006), push practitioners to understand how personal and social trauma can impact social-emotional development and sense of self. It is vital for young people to develop tools to translate experiences where they feel powerless without stripping themselves of agency. The revision can move from a stance of *what is wrong with me?* to one that simply asks, *what has happened?*

Diego makes this revision in Chapter 6, as he moves from the analogy of struggle as "dents in our frame" to struggle as fuel. This revision helped him to eventually see connections between his story and the novel alluded to in the quiz question at the opening of the chapter.

## DIFFERENTIATING REVISION

Revision took different forms for different students, although students' narrative and essay revisions tended to be interdependent. Hazel, a student featured in Chapter 4, focused on locating and shifting a specific narrative template. Abraham, featured in Chapter 5, worked to slowly reinterpret the narrative truths of his story. Diego, who is presented again in Chapter 6, put his mind to reframing a self-identified counterplot.

To evidence the range and depth of the student thinking and writing that I present in this book, I have attempted to differentiate its chapters. Chapters 2 and 3 exemplify a multiplicity of student voices and responses to the curriculum, to demonstrate the way in which student choice and differentiation were significant school gravity factors. Throughout the curriculum, students had a choice in the direction they took with topics that mattered and moved them to write. Since engagement relates to the importance students place on a task, it made sense to me to give them some control and choice in their work (Newmann, 1992; Shernoff, Csikszentmihalyi, Schneider, & Shernoff, 2003). The purpose of authentic instruction is to help students form meanings that hold genuine personal interest and relevance in the world beyond the classroom (Marks, 2000). I wanted to create opportunities to let students' internal motives drive their learning, rather than rely on a teacher-centered instructional agenda that would bypass their interior lives. By doing so, I hoped to see some of the students who appear in Chapters 2 and 3 move from peripheral to more central participation in my class.

Chapters 4, 5, and 6 portray more in-depth portraits of the students whose work was central to our curriculum's direction and to the overall class experience for almost everyone. Each of these chapters focuses almost exclusively on one student whose personal investment in learning intensified and who grew to identify more with the academic work. Hazel, Abraham, and Diego each looked penetratingly into their personal narratives and modeled what narrative revision could look like in unique ways. This helped them to develop a personal relationship with an English class and its practices and influenced their relationships with other aspects of school. Their participation was also essential to our work as a class to build a community of writers, with disciplinary identity implications for themselves and other students (Boaler & Greeno, 2000; Elbow, 1995; Lee, 2007; Reveles, Cordova, & Kelly, 2004).

Many of my students developed a deeper appreciation for the value of writing and a different understanding of what it means to be a writer. Abraham, for example, was adamant that his previous dislike for writing made him avoid it, as he explained, "Like before I was like *naw I don't wanna do this.* I wouldn't even like carrying a pencil with me." Over the spring semester, he acknowledged that his view had changed. He later expressed, "I love writing now, like I face it. I feel like I can give more details and I feel like writing is a part of life. Without writing it's like I would feel clueless." At one point, I began asking my students if they considered themselves writers. A student named Patrick replied, "Now I do. Actually, I've always considered myself a writer, but I didn't know what a writer was in school. Now I think a writer is just a person. Someone who goes through experiences and feels like people should know about them."

Hazel's written work mirrored her broadening perspectives, and she identified as a writer more than any other student. She began to recognize a connection between her writing and some changes she observed in herself. She described, "I've had a lot of moments where I'm trying to write, and I do not have words for it, and it's really frustrating. But when you do have those words, and sometimes it's just that you literally brainstorm out on a paper . . . especially when you go back you can see where you were at one point. And you see where you've changed since writing. If you continue to write, you just see the changing in it."

The changes I observed in my students lay in their writing as well as their outlook. As writers, my students grew stronger at using evidence and building arguments that served them in and out of academic contexts. They grew more comfortable considering multiple angles and perspectives. They became more inclined to pose abstract questions and contend with ambiguous answers, which improved their agility to interpret and respond analytically to various texts. Their thinking and their writing began to grow together, and their narrative and academic work began to display more writerly moves. These moves included their more deliberate, strategic attempts to state and elucidate claims, to build on their previous ideas, to compare or connect different texts, and to storytell or argue with purpose. They also began to think more like writers, as evidenced by Diego's increasing use of metaphor, Hazel's repetition of key themes and phrases, and the vocabulary of narrative constructs that began to emerge in their academic work. Maizie, who is presented in Chapter 3, described her development of a writer's consciousness, "It was me growing, as a person and as a writer . . . once you get into it you get into more and more and more, like there's more things to talk about, it's not just one thing, because one thing leads to another. . . . I mean it could be anything but as long as it's real. But there's always something that connects to you. If you love writing, somehow some way it connects to you."

Many of my students learned to connect more critically with their stories and to engage with the stories of others. Some of their revisions helped them find more stable states of mind, which in turn helped them steady themselves and their relationships. At the end of the semester, Hazel stated, "I think people can see the change . . . I think our shoulders are just more up, like I think we just know more. You don't feel so lost anymore, you just feel more wholesome. And it's way more peaceful, instead of just going around like *why me, why me, why me,* now it's just like *aaahhhhh.*"

As a teacher, I learned the importance of listening to students' views and taking their reticence toward school seriously. Research shows that students are sometimes more inclined to respect school when teachers are willing to acknowledge and accept their negative reactions to parts of their experience (Reeve, Jang, Carrell, Jeon, & Barch, 2004). Yazzie-Mintz and McCormick note that "listening to students about their schooling experiences is not a new concept, just an infrequently invoked one" (2012, p. 757). Rather than criticizing students' views, we can work to change the associations and meanings young people may have about what it means to be a student. This means building opportunities for them to realize that their personal, cultural, and academic identities can grow in congruence (Ladson-Billings, 1995). This book is an attempt to show how a literacy curriculum that intertwines personal and academic engagement and builds around the theme of love can push students toward this goal.

The relationships that my class and I formed as a learning community, as we became active participants in one another's lives, were invaluable to this mission—as Diego explained at the end of his junior year, "Teachers learning with students is the best school gravity there is."

## CHAPTER 2

# Writing Love

**Love:** *noun*.1. A fantasy. 2. Not loneliness, rejection, or losing someone. 3. The most wonderful thing any human being can receive. 4. Desire to have. 5. Pain. 6. Something I push away. 7. An attachment. 8. Something essential to heal an emotional wound. 9. The one thing that can keep us together. 10. A pleasant thing that you liked when your family gave it to you or a shitty feeling when growing up was a painful experience. For everybody it's different. 11. I don't really know.

—Original Definitions, 11th Grade English

I chose to place love at the center of our curriculum because of its potential to critically engage students with their stories and to build a rich dialogue that connected them thematically to literary analysis and academic work. I also hoped to appeal to their social-emotional intelligence—and their desire to be resilient—to draw them into conversation about literature and writing and their relationships with school. The topic of love held school gravity for my students because it treated their social-emotional intelligence as a valid strength. Several students expressed that this helped to make school more meaningful. A student named Alisha, who is presented in Chapter 3, explained, "It just makes you think about life and school, and certain things in school, how some of it can help you."

School is traditionally a place where we are "taught to believe that the mind, not the heart, is the seat of learning" (hooks, 2000, p. xxvii). Daniel Goleman notes that our steady focus on raising academic standards does little to build students' emotional literacy. He argues that "academic intelligence offers virtually no preparation for the turmoil—or opportunity—life's vicissitudes bring. . . . Our schools and our culture fixate on academic abilities, ignoring *emotional* intelligence, a set of traits—some might call it character—that also matters immensely for our personal destiny" (1995, p. 36). Emotional intelligence is conceptualized broadly as the ability to know and recognize emotional responses in others and ourselves and to use this awareness effectively (Goleman, 1995; Mayer & Salovey, 1997). Goleman stresses that our "inability to monitor our true feelings leaves us at their mercy. People with greater certainty about their feelings are better pilots of their lives" (p. 43).

Serenity, introduced in the previous chapter, spoke to this point when she observed in conversation with me that her emotional confidence and well-being were factors that steered her thinking. She described, "If I could have helped myself out mentally before, maybe I would have cared about keeping control of my life instead of letting people take it from me or handing it off."

## WHY LOVE? BECOMING LOVE LITERATE

The school gravity of writing love emerged in specific elements of the curriculum that I elucidate in this chapter. One pull factor was the way in which students' narratives about love embodied their life outlooks and understandings of change. Another was the extent to which their narratives incorporated literary elements that connected in consequential ways to their well-being and emerged in their writing as evocative substance for further contemplation. The strategy of sharing our writing with one another—including writing that I shared—became another pull factor and a constructive means to explore our lives as texts. As a student named Maizie expressed, "Like how you did it, it was like life lessons and then trying to get us to learn how to write better. . . . It shows us something about us and something about school."

The topic of love was central to my students' self-stories. Their attempts to make sense of love in their lives influenced their sense of purpose. Yet the majority of my students struggled to pinpoint a definitive meaning of love and either began or ended their papers with this disclaimer. One student opened with the lines, "The dictionary has 11 different definitions for love. That's an example of how no one really knows what love is." Another admitted, "Love is a very strong word that many of us really don't know what it means. . . . I'd honestly rather be writing about war just because it's easier. Writing about love is complicated." Another student revealed, "Lost is the only word that comes to mind when trying to realize the meaning of love." One student ended her paper with the words, "In conclusion I really don't know what love is."

My students' confusion about the meaning of love seemed to undermine their sense of agency to create or achieve love in their lives. It is tough to build into our lives what we struggle to imagine or define, as bell hooks reminds us in *All About Love*, "Definitions are vital starting points for the imagination. What we cannot imagine cannot come into being" (2000, p. 14). My students' definitions of love indicated a struggle to imagine themselves with means to confront or surmount what troubled them. Their reticence to define love hit at the core of their sense of personal and academic competence and—in some cases—worth.

Many of my students held expectations for their school and life success based on personal beliefs about their adequacy as people and students. Writing love asked them to explore how these beliefs had potential impact on the lives they were building, both in and out of the classroom. Goleman (1995) identifies the five core competencies of emotional literacy as self-awareness, social awareness and empathetic capacity, self-motivation, self-management, and social and relationship skills. All of these connected to my students' capacities to sustain a productive focus in school. Abraham observed that his academic focus depended on his emotional state of mind, explaining to me that "anger would come . . . and then I would take it out towards school. And then my grades would be affected because I wouldn't care about my grades." Serenity made a similar point about her self-awareness, noting that "not knowing who you are really does affect how you handle situations. . . . You don't know how to handle it if you don't know where you stand."

The process of writing love integrated my students' academic and social-emotional learning and required them to blend cognitive and social-emotional skills. Joseph Zins and Maurice Elias (2006) emphasize the integration of these skills as essential to effective curriculum and pedagogy. They argue that academic achievement and social-emotional competence are interwoven to the extent that "integrated, coordinated instruction in both areas maximizes students' potential to succeed in school and in life" (p. 233). A combination of academic and emotional intelligence was necessary for the writing assignments in our curriculum, and my goal was for my students to increasingly care about caring—to combine metacognition and meta-emotion—so, as Thomas Likona describes, they "come to feel deeply about what they think and value" (1991, p. 151).

My students' initial narratives revealed associations with love in their lives that were metaphorical for their life outlooks. The act of *writing* about love, rather than discussing or reading about it, helped them to see more tangibly where they stood in their views. Abraham explained, "I guess like, I can't see myself when I'm going through it but then when I put it on paper I can actually see my feelings. . . . When I'm writing about it, like I actually think about it." I asked my students to write about love so they could see their narratives and essays as rhetorical projections of themselves. Over time, I wanted them to see changes in their thinking that emerged as evidence in writing, so they could identify when their life outlooks shaped their words, and vice versa.

My goal was not so much that students would turn in polished writing on the first paper, but that they would write to learn, remember, dialogue with themselves, and start to figure out what they did not know. I wanted them to write as active learners who were processing ideas, developing a sense of their minds, and beginning to find their own language, analogies, and metaphors (Elbow, 1997). These goals also guided my feedback, which was primarily descriptive. I described to students what I heard them say and do, since, as Peter Elbow explains, "one of the hardest things for student writers is to simply *see* their own text" (1997, p. 10). I shared my observations of their reasoning, main points, assumptions, and evidence, and my perceptions of their overall message. I also wrote my metacognitive thoughts that occurred as I read. As Elbow argues, "It is a mark of respect to students when we take *what* they write seriously enough to reply with our thoughts on the

topic—instead of just making metacomments on how well they have written"
(2000, p. 31). This connected to a comment that Diego made: "It's easier for
students to write papers if you're real about reading the papers. Like I've
known some teachers that you just turn in an essay and they would be like
*oh no paragraphs, oh he scribbles all over, you know what, go and type this
up and give me a real essay.* And I'll be like *fuck you.*"

Descriptive feedback can offer students some distance and perspective
on their work (Elbow & Belanoff, 2000). Another of my goals was to convey
what I understood. Elbow notes, "Isn't this what makes us and our students
want to continue to write? To be understood is more rewarding than to be
praised. Being understood is what makes us want to take the trouble to
articulate more of what is on our minds" (2000, pp. 31–32). I pointed out
moves students made that may not have been intentional, to help them grow
more conscious as writers. I also attempted to engage with their thinking and
writing in what Elbow (1973) calls the "believing game." Rather than solely
critique or debate the content and quality of their work, I tried to listen, af-
firm, coax, and coach. This does not mean there was no place for evaluation.
I worked with my class on topics such as organization and citation, and with
different students on various grammar structures that were struggles for them.
However, as Elbow explains, "believing" means "entering in . . . understanding
ideas from the inside . . . the believing game is particularly useful for eliciting
and understanding ideas that are the limits of what we can imagine or explain"
(2000, p. 77). My commitment to play the believing game throughout the
curriculum, and read *with* students rather than *against* them, was essential
to their will to take risks and write honestly.

Another pedagogical strategy I used extensively was the writing confer-
ence. In our conferences—or conversations, as I call them—my students and
I would sit down one-on-one or in small groups and take turns reading their
writing out loud so they could really *hear* their meaning and grammar. From
a grammatical standpoint, I aimed for what Mike Rose describes as "[dealing]
with specific bits of language . . . [shuttling] back and forth between print and
voice, making me breathe my prose, making me hear the language I'd gener-
ated in silence" (1989, p. 55). This method helped students to grasp different
options or changes in syntax or wording that could lend them the rhythm
and meaning they were going for. From the standpoint of meaning, I drew
on a process called *stimulated elicitation* (Odell, Goswami, & Herrington,
1983), in which I took various courses of questioning to ask students to tell
me more about the meaning of their work. Sometimes I pointed to specific
lines and asked them to describe what they had written or to elaborate on
it. Sometimes I asked if they could perceive connections between different
parts of a paper or different pieces of their writing. Sometimes I asked them
to talk specifically about themes they could see emerging in their writing or
to identify ideas or issues that they were trying to work out over the course
of multiple papers. Sometimes I asked them to talk more generally about

how they perceived themselves as writers or how they thought of school in relation to their lives. My aim in these conversations was to gain deeper understanding of how my students made sense of their writing, how they approached their writing processes, and how they experienced the curriculum and school. It was also an opportunity for them to reflect on their personal and academic development.

## LOVE METAPHORS AND LIFE OUTLOOKS

Several students articulated in their writing the understanding that love did not exist. One student stated plainly, "I don't think there is such a thing as love," while another wrote, "What love is to me is a fantasy. I say that love with your boyfriend or girlfriend does not exist." Another student was emphatic in his assertion that "[love] is bullshit, there is no such thing. Just something you hope is there but never is." As I read and responded to these narratives, I asked students to think deeply about why they were denying love. I asked them to think about how their views reflected a belief in their ability to create a quality of life they wanted. This led our class to consider the perception that some aspects of life are beyond our control and how this differs from the view that life is altogether fated.

Some students expressed contradictory impulses to reject love even when, on a deeper level, they wanted to embrace it. One student wrote, "Why in my head I have love framed as a good thing for people to have, but I push it away at any hint of having it?" Others felt that personal rejection was an inevitable consequence of loving others. Kylie, whose work is presented in Chapter 3, described love as a perpetual story of defeat, arguing, "One day Jamie Marie's fantasy of love will come true. Not! Who are you kidding. Love is complicated. It will last for a while then die down." I also noticed that some students were careful to distinguish love from rejection or "pain that's carved into your memory that can scar you for life. . . . I think if it hurts to remember, then it's not love at all." One student wrote, "Everyone says that love hurts, but that's not true. Loneliness hurts, rejection hurts, losing someone hurts. Everyone confuses these with love." The difference in these arguments raised a question for our class: What were the implications for outlooks that equated love with pain versus those that distinguished love from negative emotions?

Diego was one of several students who described love as a no-win situation. He wrote, "Why do people love the people that don't love them, and don't love the people that do love them? There is really nothing attractive about being pathetic over someone." This view echoed to me what a student had written when I asked my class to describe in writing the disconnect they perceived from school: "Some people just think that if they are in the hole already they can't get out and they are scared to try again because their mind is set that they are a failure. And they don't know how to change their mind." The sense of futility he expressed seemed relevant to my students' instincts to resist terms that were not theirs by opting out and validating "failure" as the inevitable outcome.

Writing about love raised issues tied to many of my students' adolescent anxieties. For most of them, the topic surfaced more than trivial concerns. It engaged them with questions that were developmentally complex, and the level of challenge added to the school gravity of the curriculum. Researchers believe that the life story "takes flight" in adolescence (McAdams, 1993), with the emergence of formal operational thinking and identity strivings that push young people to question and contemplate their realities and personal truths (Erikson, 1968; Habermas & Bluck, 2000; Piaget, 1968). The love narratives stretched developmental capacities that were present but relatively new. For example, writing about love asked my students to consider the interrelation between their previous and past selves and the coexistence of personal continuity and change (Guardo & Bohan, 1971; Habermas & Bluck, 2000; Mohr, 1978). This connects to Erikson's description of identity construction as a "subjective sense of an invigorating sameness and continuity" (1968, p. 19). Writing love also pushed my students to identify and assess thematic repetition in their lives and to conceptualize of change as a process rather than a product (Dreher & Dreher, 1991; Habermas & Bluck, 2000). Over the course of the curriculum, the writing assignments pushed students to hypothesize, reflect, theorize, project, and interpret their experience. Piaget's (1968) description of formal operational thinking lays the groundwork for these requisite capacities. They are synonymous with what Erikson claims are essential for adolescent identity formation, which he describes as "simultaneous reflection and observation . . . taking place on all levels of mental functioning" (1968, pp. 22–23).

Returning to Diego's point, "Why I think a lot of kids don't change is because I don't think you realize how big of a change you're asking," writing love offered students a chance to address the process of change in a real way. It seemed fair—and most effective—to help them understand that personal change is a *process* rather than to ask for change in their engagement or behavior without acknowledging the scope of this request. Personal change is complicated, regardless of age. Memory research shows that our self-memory system is structurally designed to make enduring, intrapersonal change a difficult and painful process (Conway, Singer, & Tagini, 2004). Daniel Schacter, in *The Seven Sins of Memory* (2001), argues that our theories of self and the world influence how we select and encode memories, which makes it difficult to write stories that fly in the face of how we see ourselves. Change requires us to withstand the cognitive and affective stress that accompanies an internal reconfiguration of schemata and narrative scripts in our long-term memory (Conway et al., 2004; Tomkins, 1987). In other words, we have to deviate from a familiar story and learn to interpret and contextualize our encounters with the world in a way that is *inconsistent* with the narrative we have been writing all along.

I wanted my students to contemplate changes to some of the understandings and outlooks that emerged in their love narratives. However, a classroom community was needed to support this effort and lend school gravity to work that was exceptionally hard. Toni Morrison describes the approach that I was aiming for:

> In personal life, you have to know what happened and why and figure it out, and then you can go onto another level freer, stronger, tempered in some way. Constantly burying it, distorting it, and pretending, I think, is unhealthy. (Denard, 2008, p. 129)

To replace avoidance with the desire to "figure it out," my students needed to engage with one another's stories, so they could begin to see them as possibilities within a myriad of ways to interpret the world and assess their creative power in it.

## SHARED WRITING: "YOU REALIZE YOU'RE NOT ALONE"

When the very meaning of the word is cloaked in mystery, it should not come as a surprise that most people find it hard to define what they mean when they use the word 'love.' . . . Imagine how much easier it would be for us to learn how to love if we began with a shared definition.

—bell hooks, All About Love

I endeavored to build a community of writers through a pedagogical strategy that began with sharing anonymous excerpts of student work. To develop identities as writers, my students needed access to each other's thinking to develop deeper insights into their own. Peter Elbow argues for this kind of dialogue, stating, "I encourage students to situate what they write into the conversation of other members of the classroom community to whom they are writing and whom they are reading" (1995, p. 79). I highlighted excerpts from student papers as I read them, selecting those that struck me as symbolic or generative or that exemplified expressive or enticing uses of language. Then I typed them anonymously into a class handout that I distributed when I returned their writing, and we read it aloud as a class. I often asked students to respond by journaling to lines their classmates had written. Over time, they became used to this process and would request these handouts because they wanted to see what others had said. Hazel, whose work is featured in Chapter 4, commented, "At first you're nervous when we get to the line that's yours, but then you look around the room and see people nodding to what you wrote, and you realize you're not alone. Or you read where someone wrote something you feel the same about."

The list below shows the handout that we created from students' initial love narratives. After we read this text aloud, I asked students to further engage with it through an inductive thinking process. I had them cut apart the different lines, sort them into groups that they felt shared common themes, and identify and name the themes about love that emerged in our class. This led into a discussion of narrative templates described in Chapter 3.

Anonymous Quotes from Student Love Papers

The dictionary has 11 different definitions for love. That's an example of how no one really knows what love is.

Everyone says that love hurts, but that's not true. Loneliness hurts, rejection hurts, losing someone hurts. Everyone confuses these with love . . .

Love is the most wonderful thing any human being can receive. Just feeling wanted by someone, and being noticed by someone makes a difference to how you feel inside.

Some people doubt all love. They seem to think just because their relationship didn't work they can bring others down about it . . . some of them seem to think "oh I broke up, that means they are too," or "my relationship didn't work, theirs isn't going to either," or "oh he's this way, that's how my ex was, all men are the same."

It's crazy to see people start to cry when they start to sad trip over old relationships. I think if it hurts to remember, then it's not love at all. It's just pain, pain that's carved into your memory that can scar you for life.

My mom—the love you have for her is the love you can't explain. It's the kind of feeling you can't express or say out loud because you just want to keep it to yourself and cherish the way she is with you . . . that's why I think a mother's love is greater than any other love. There's another love I can't explain because I've never had it and that's my father's love. My mom told me that his parents never showed him love.

I believe love makes you naïve. Love makes you act like a complete fool. Naïve in the way you know he lies, you know the words that come out of his mouth aren't true. But you choose to believe the lie.

Very soon the life you live is a lie. You avoid the truth because the truth hurts. The rude behavior that you wish goes away, doesn't. So you make an excuse. At the end you don't end up respecting yourself. Sometimes at the end of a relationships you ask yourself, "why didn't I respect my mind and body." You think back did I really love him. Sometimes it's just hard to walk away. You believe the guy you're with is right for you. You want to be the girl he loves.

Is love always balanced? If not then is it love or obsession? Is obsession a bad thing when it just means you want to surround yourself with the one you love?

What love is to me is a fantasy.

It's clearly something everyone wants because the purpose of it is something essential to heal an emotional wound. A purpose that goes far beyond my thinking capability.

Memories of _____ were everywhere I looked.

Love before for me was just a bunch of b.s. I would leave a girl when she started to fall for me. I would do this because I didn't want to be emotionally attached to someone. I was scared to feel love for someone. I would see people that would get all sad when they would break up and I didn't want to feel that, . . . Nowadays love for me is a different thing. I have felt the pain that I always had dread of. Now that I have felt this pain I'm kind of glad that I have.

I see her coming, when she pass my way now, not lust just beauty I feel blessed today now . . .

I love love.

Aside from disclosing to students that there were others who "wrote something you feel the same about," these mentor texts had several goals. One was to lend school gravity to the writing assignments by inviting the few students who were hesitant to try them to engage with their classmates' work. I hoped this would compel them to join and participate in the class conversation (and hopefully the writing) by showing them that the work had value. I also wanted to encourage the growth of community. As Parker Palmer notes, "Community emerges when we are willing to share the real concerns of our lives" (1999, p. 6). The extent to which students felt a genuine part of our classroom community influenced their desire and comfort to share their writing and learn from one another. Christenson and Havsy observe that "motivation is heightened when students feel they are heard and respected" (2004, p. 66), and the practice of sharing writing helped students to develop a sense of ownership and accomplishment that was integral to their engagement.

Another goal of the student mentor texts was to create a classroom space that allowed for what Bakhtin (1981) calls "dialogization," or the rendering of imaginable stories through their encounter with possible alternate tellings. Genishi and Dyson (1994) contend that students' stories warrant space in the classroom precisely because it is a site where this possibility may emerge. They explain, "If stories . . . are never echoed or challenged in stories heard in the classroom forum—they will never be 'dialogized,' to use Bakhtin's term. That is, they will not be rendered a story among possible stories, other ways of being" (p. 5). I wanted to engage students with their writing so they could see their stories as constructed and more consciously recognize choices they made in construction. In Morrison's words, I wanted them to "know what happened and why and figure it out," since, as she argues, "evading it is a sure way to have a truncated life, a life that has no possibilities in it" (Denard, 2008, p. 129). This dialogization required students to weigh their accounts with others and let their stories be challenged in a community forum.

For this process to work, I needed my students to take their texts seriously as potential templates for their lives. This meant that I needed to treat their writing with the same status and respect as the scholarly or "expert" texts that I shared with them through the English curriculum. The method would miss the mark if I privileged writing from outside of the classroom and disregarded what students wrote as less valuable. Despite obvious differences in my students' abilities and experiences with writing compared to established writers, they needed to see their texts as important and *real* in the way of those by authors I asked them to read. In *Textual Power*, Robert Scholes argues that "we must stop 'teaching literature' and start 'studying texts.' . . . All kinds of texts . . . must be taken as occasions for further textuality" (1985, p. 16). Through sharing students' writing, I endeavored to present their texts to them as quality material for literary and life analysis. I essentially used *their writing* to engage them with writing, along with their personal and academic questions that tied to personal and academic texts.

## LOVE'S LITERARY ELEMENTS

To help my students appreciate their narratives as objects of study, I focused them on specific literary elements—setting, tone, plot, theme, characters, and defenses—to engage them with the content of their stories and their craft of writing them. I drew their attention to these elements as I read and commented on their papers and met with them to discuss their work. My purpose was to build school gravity into the personal narratives and to give students tools along with the impetus to engage with the rich substance of their stories and lives. Eventually, I used the literary elements I define in this section to engage students with the characters' narratives in the literary text. I wanted them to see that we were not reading into these literary elements as a pointless academic exercise, but because they matter to our happiness and well-being.

As students began to explore how they storied "what happened and why," as Morrison describes, I realized that they had embedded clues in different literary elements that I could ask them to examine. These literary elements provided them with entry points into their writing and stories. For example, Kylie's first love narrative evoked a fairy tale setting that caught my attention. McAdams (1993) and Singer (2005) define the setting of a life story as a state of mind and a set of beliefs that we bring to most stories we write. In Kylie's writing, she created a section called "Storytime" that began, "Once upon a time there was a beautiful princess named Jamie Marie. She was young but not too young. She always wondered what love was." Kylie's setting implied that love was not possible, except in a fantasy world where she had control over what she could create. One challenge for her as she thought about her story was to reflect on why her setting took this form.

The setting contextualizes our tone, or the internal voice that conveys our outlook and the emotional subtexts of our thinking. Students' narrative tones were rife with meaning. Many of them found it useful to notice this and to assess the emotions their tones carried or the thoughts underneath. Several students acknowledged that the tone in their writing was indicative of the voice that emerged when they dialogued internally with themselves.

Diego defined love as struggle in his initial narrative, and his paper *felt* like a struggle to read. It wrestled with circuitous questions and arguments that had no resolution, and his tone was pessimistic and angry, as he wrote, "Why don't we all just be assholes? Then everyone will love you. Be the guy that people want but no one has. That would be fucking great. Except if you're not the asshole that everyone wants, you're the nice one that people walk over. Why does being nice get confused with being weak?"

Abraham's tone was angry but carried more self-contempt. It was also apologetic, as though it lacked validation. He wrote, "I wish this feeling fades away, it's building like a box of hate. Everytime I want tell you I love you, I hesitate. Sometimes I wish I was never made, Lord please erase my birthdate. If I had the choice to change my identity I would just to make my family happy."

Hazel's tone, in contrast, was the most open and vulnerable. Her setting was one of mixed emotions—sadness and beauty combined—and her outlook strove for optimism and acceptance of herself and others. She wrote, "People I've known for only a short briefness in my life have showed me so much love, and the people I've known forever give it to me in slim pickens. Though how can I go without loving love? I love love."

She observed in her second love narrative, presented in Chapter 4, that her tone changed as she went deeper into her story. She self-assessed her tone as one that alternated between dominance and fear, and she tied these oscillations to a pattern that she perceived in her actions. She wrote, "I'm trying to break the cycle right now because it always ends up making me fight or hurt myself. When I think of this subject my tone feels anxious, stressed, in control, dominant, weak, angry, and scared. I get confident at first, fall in love with dominance and control. Then about a year goes by. I started to feel anxious and disempowered by my own impulsive temptations. Then about a year and a half goes by and I start to feel weak."

A key point of school gravity was to ask students to observe how they chose to story themselves as characters in their writing and the potential implications of this portrayal. Most of them had not previously considered this connection. Diego characterized himself in his narrative as a fighter in a futile struggle. This, he later realized, tended to lead him to moments of defeat that he had grown to anticipate. Kylie wrote herself as a target for maltreatment who was unable to take control when situations escalated. This was a pattern she later identified in her narrative template. Abraham storied himself as illegitimate. He also wrote about people in his life who held symbolic roles in his story. His initial love narrative pointed to a character named "MA," who represented a voice of rejection. McAdams argues that our stories develop with implicit listeners in mind, since the nature of stories is to be told (McAdams, 1996). Part of Abraham's narrative work in later papers was to edit this voice that had become an internalized audience and pervaded his thinking. Hazel's writing also included important characters, and she wrote about both of her parents across multiple love narratives. Her academic essays developed a similar focus on how the parents in *Song of Solomon* embodied their roles. The focus of her narrative work was a revision of the roles her parents played as characters in her life.

The themes that emerged in students' writing developed from personal questions that arose in their love narratives and guided their thinking over the next several papers. McAdams (1993) defines a theme as a recurrent undertone that reflects unresolved desires or points to patterns in our experiences. The literary elements of theme and plot are interrelated, in that thematic repetition tends to comprise the core subject matter of cyclical plotlines. Plots are the narrative arcs that give the story a direction. They are interpretive rather than objective, meaning that actual events are less significant than the symbolic role they come to play in our stories.

In our class, the narrative themes we identified through shared writing became a primary focus of the curriculum. Several thematic associations with love began to emerge in students' love narratives, including *love is pain*, *love is self-love*, and *love is struggle*. Kylie argued that love cannot be reciprocal because it is grounded in unequal control. Hazel claimed that we are able to love others to the extent that we love ourselves, but she was unable to define self-love. Abraham's first narrative was cryptic and revolved around his statement, "I hate the truth." He did not reveal what "the truth" was, but he connected it to a theme of rejection. Diego, on the other hand, argued that love is struggle.

These themes helped my students interpret their own writing and connect their papers over the course of the curriculum.

An element that is not traditionally associated with literary analysis but was integral to our self-narrative work is that of *defense*. Defenses have power to shape the life story, and McAdams argues that they function to make "some stories more tellable than they might otherwise be and to keep other potentially storied accounts from reaching the status of ever being told" (1998, p. 1127). For Kylie, her claim that love did not exist was a defense. Diego's defenses were a justification that love's futility relieves us of some accountability. Abraham alluded to a story that he was not telling and offered self-eradication as the resolution. Hazel, in contrast, was able to identify some of her defenses and write explicitly about them. While she never defined the self-love that was missing, she expressed later in reflection, "This paper *made* me notice I didn't love myself."

My students' defenses shaped their writing as well as the coping mechanisms they used in school. I wanted to discuss the element of defense so we could talk candidly as a class about how defenses marked their relationships with school and their ways of engaging. I wanted to legitimize reasons why defenses form as a response to life. I also wanted to emphasize that there are times when our defenses are needed and times when they sabotage us.

Our class focus on these literary elements helped students begin to realize where they had choices in their interpretation of their lives and their story construction. As students read each other's papers and witnessed different ways of writing love, they began to try harder to figure out their own. As Hazel wrote, "We're broken little pieces playing games with ourselves. The love's there, it might be hard to find but it's the one thing that can keep us together. One love."

## MY NARRATIVE WORK: WRITING TO "FACE IT"

I wish to note that my story made its way into the mix of writing we shared. My methods included my decision to engage with my students in their narrative work and participate in assignments that I asked them to do. This meant sharing subjective pieces of my family history, along with excerpts of my writing, and offering my story as a case of writing and rewriting love to better exemplify how and why this work mattered.

My original definition of love was incubated in the instability that emanated from the mental illness that pervaded both sides of my family and marked the first 18 years of my life. My mother's illness, and her inability to express love in healthy or nurturing ways, had the closest impact on me. I decided to disclose this story to my students when I read their definitions of love and found myself making countless connections. One student included lines about our first associations with love that stretch across our lives: "Your brain is like a sponge that soaks in information and for love it is like the same way. Either love was a pleasant thing that you liked when your family gave it to you or it was a shitty feeling when growing up was a painful experience. For everybody it's different but your early stages of life determine your viewpoint on what love is." These lines registered with me because I knew that it had taken me a while as an adult to understand this concept. This was precisely the kind of conversation I had needed as an adolescent, but it wasn't the type of thing I had discussed in high school.

I suppose these realizations prompted me to explore my story with students. Moreover, I recognized that they were personalizing problems in their lives that were not directly about them and were on a much larger human scale than they realized. I had done something similar. I was well into my adult life before I tried to exorcise some unwarranted explanations that had woven their way into my "viewpoint on what love is," as my student expressed.

Before I met the students in this book, I attempted to align pieces of my father's story with mine. It became a paper that I submitted for a graduate class on history, memory, and trauma. I felt I could better convey the concept of writing love, and get my students to care about it, if I kept working on this narrative and shared it with them. My intent was to show them the school gravity of the process—at any age—and illustrate how my father and I each used writing to reach deeper realizations about where our stories came from.

I knew little or nothing about my father's family or his early life until he began writing his life story a few years after my mother died and a few years before his death. He sent me 90 typed pages through the U.S. mail that I typed into my computer and saved. In the paper that I wrote for my class, I tried to juxtapose sections of my story with his, like James McBride does with alternate chapters of his and his mother's stories in *The Color of Water*. It was the first time that either of us had attempted to tell our stories to anyone. He was 80 and I was 33.

One reason for our silent internalization was that our stories were difficult to tell, since the intimacies of living with mental illness can be difficult to convey and easily misunderstood. When I was my students' age, I watched my mother deal with borderline personality disorder. Throughout my adolescence, she remained unable to confront what troubled her and pushed away others' support. You can see her illness manifest in her expression in the photo in Figure 2.1. I'm sitting on my aunt's lap, with my mother on the left.

Patients with borderline personality disorder suffer from self-destructive actions and constantly shifting emotions marked by intense anger, despair, feelings of emptiness, and fears of abandonment. More than most of us, they struggle to maintain close interpersonal relationshps. They tend to polarize their worlds, alternately idealizing and devaluing those who love them, while continuously wounding and feeling wounded by those in their lives who matter most (Gunderson, 2009; Van Gelder, 2010).

**Figure 2.1. Family Photo, Includes My Aunt and Uncle, Grandma, Mom, and Me**

Borderline personality disorder did not enter the American Psychiatric Association's Diagnostic and Statistical Manual of Mental Disorders until 1980. It remains under-researched and highly stigmatized despite the estimate that it affects 6% of the population. Project Borderline, an organization created by Brandon Marshall (2012), an NFL player who was diagnosed in 2011 and became a national spokesman for the illness, paints a description of the paradox that underlies its competing storylines: "Although borderline personality disorder is usually identified by impulsive behaviors and highly emotional outbursts, many clinicians believe that the condition primarily reflects a profound sensitivity to relationships. . . . This instability is played out in how they experience the people in their lives." My understanding of love reflects this instability, along with my evolving effort to process and story the confusing initial experience of feeling simultaneously needed and despised, alternately all-consumed and rejected, and labeled "good" and profoundly "bad" in the same narrative.

My work to resolve these competing messages formed the substance of two papers that I shared with students. One was my narrative template, in which I identified a storyline that resonated in different aspects of my life. It depicted a familiar form of love to me, and as I explained to students, it created a "comfort zone" that was not a comfortable place. I also wanted my students to understand that I played a role every time this dynamic repeated in my life. It was not something others did to me. My ability to reconfigure this story tied to how I chose to make sense of it, which was the focus of the second paper I shared with them later.

**Figure 2.2. My Love Template**

1. My mom and I. Our relationship is about HER needs. She needs someone who needs her and who does not have identity outside of her. My needs, to her, do not exist because she's unable to consider them or think outside of her own perspective.
2. I show signs of breaking away, of being my own person, of thinking independently. I think about MY needs. She can't handle this because she takes it as personal rejection.
3. She punishes me. HARD. I don't know what I did wrong, exactly, but I know I triggered something.
4. We go through a period of separation. Isolation. Not speaking. Not interacting. No real contact. No communication.
5. Out of nowhere she "shows up" for the relationship and acts like "mom," like everything's normal. I *want* a mom, so I take her back, no questions asked.

Figure 2.2 shows the storyboard portion of the writing that I paired with a narrative that was several pages long, which is not presented here.

Until I read my father's writing, it never made sense to me why his definition of love compelled him to accept my mother's volatile behavior as normal or why he enabled her illness to the extent that he did. It was hard for me to grasp why he turned a blind eye on the abuse of his five children and treated the insecurity and pain in our lives as something familiar.

Then I found two pages in my father's writing that struck me because they portrayed what was clearly his mother's mental illness. He had never spoken of it. I imagine that he wrote about it because he did not know how else to share it. I am not sure that he thought it was okay to discuss. Towards the end of his life, writing became a way that he could access himself and the stories that he was otherwise unable to convey.

My father was born in upstate New York a few weeks before the stock market crash of 1928, and his parents lost their farm in the Great Depression. His mother began to clean homes, and his father became the local fire chief of Whitehall. They moved 11 times in 16 years, when he was between the ages of 3 and 18. In his writing, shown in Figure 2.3, he explains the reason for this.

When I learned to understand my father instead of blame him, it marked the beginning of my narrative work.

My father's writing gave me the material I needed for my story revision. Prior to reading his work, I did not understand what form of love was familiar to him, or why. Afterwards, I was able to connect his story to mine. I shared this connection with my students because I wanted them think about the missing pieces in their stories, and how they could explore them in a way that would allow them to rewrite love with deeper understanding.

I did not share my father's text with my students. I did share my response to it, whereby I attempted a graphic novel style of writing that used photos

### Figure 2.3. My Father's Writing

The problem was that my mother developed a phobia about dead rats or mice. Alive, they were annoying pests, but they were not the source of her fears. Dead, they were a painful obsession.

At some point after moving to the village, my mother's phobia became all-consuming and controlling. Furthermore, it was not just the presence or feared presence of the dead animal. What was even more damaging in her mind was the perceived contamination of space that a decaying rat or mouse caused through its exposure to a part of the house. And it was only these animals. Other dead animals had no effect on her.

Once she thought she detected the telltale odor of a decaying mouse in the partitions of a house, she eliminated our use of the space and any contents that she felt the odor had contaminated. Rooms, parts of rooms, and their contents thereof were left to collect dust, and we could not use or touch them under penalty of causing intense emotional pain for the whole family. This fear of finding the dreaded odor pervaded her life for that fifteen or sixteen years. It eliminated any stability in our family life.

Our family never entered a house without the subconscious fear that my mother would decide she smelled a dead mouse. Then the sequence would begin of trying to comfort her fears and dissuade her—never successfully that I can remember—and survive, until we found a way to accommodate the limitations she placed on house space—or else began the process of moving again. When the houses we lived in had bedroom space for Joe and me, it usually became "contaminated" to the degree that I don't remember us ever having our own room. Likewise, my parents slept on sofa-beds in the living room, while bedroom space was available but off limits.

---

instead of illustrations. The idea came to me because of my mother's obsession with cameras. She took photos in a manner that is hard to explain unless you happened to be the focus of them. She genuinely believed that everyone whom she loved abandoned her, even as she compulsively pushed them away. Photos were her way of preserving the people in her life. This is how we ended up with a basement stashed with boxes of photos that most people in my family had never seen. We would ask to see copies of the pictures sometimes, but even when she tried to find them for us, she almost never knew where they were. They got lost in the recesses of our house, which, over the years, began to physically resemble the recesses of her mind. In my narrative, I interspersed my writing with the photos that I salvaged after her death, and I added hand-written captions as commentary.

This work arises partly from the fact that healing was not my family's mantra. Negative incidents with doctors led us to distrust psychology and to consider psychiatry a bogus profession. They also led us to repel the work of critical self-reflection. We were intensely skeptical of the complexion of ideas

**Figure 2.4. My Memoir**

My mother was obsessed with taking photographs. She took photos of
people and places everywhere she went. She did not have any formal
training in photography. So her pictures were full of thumbs,

and people who were cut off at the head or waist,

and people who were not centered or stuck off to the side somewhere.

### Figure 2.4. My Memoir

But she also captured some amazing impressions.

*This was at the beach of Lake Michigan.*

My mother didn't take photos the way people do for a hobby. She took photos because she couldn't bear the thought of leaving a moment behind. She couldn't let go. Her determination to guard people and events in her life forever was the main source of her sense of control in the world. She didn't like to have her picture taken, though, which explains why she is usually the person in the family who is not shown.

*In Sacramento. My brothers had hitchhiked there and I'm holding the "Oregon" sign.*

*(Continued)*

**Figure 2.4. My Memoir**

It also explains why, in so many photos, we appear to be glaring at the camera.

*Lots of photos of eating.*

The irony was that we rarely saw the photos after she took them. While my mother was alive, she kept them buried in boxes, under beds, in the basement, and in closets. It turned out that she was as protective of the photos as she was of the events she tried to capture. She tried desperately to hang on to both.

*My other brother Craig.*

It is only after her death that I have gone through her boxes and found most of these photos. I have decided that it is important to put them to use.

**Figure 2.4. My Memoir**

---

I love these photos of when she was young. You can't see her illness . . .

So now the world can see them.

that underlie this book. I believe this cynicism has obstructed our ability to know each other, which has impeded our individual healing. It is increasingly apparent to me that our reluctance to understand our definitions of love has made us immune to some of life's joys. Toni Morrison touches on this point when she says that the purpose of her novels is not to present our inheritance as "a terrible palm or fist that pounds everybody to death, but to have happiness or growth represented in the way in which people deal with their past, which means they have to come to terms, confront it, sort it out" (Denard, 2008, pp. 128–129). This is the spirit with which I approached my students, and it is the spirit with which I write.

While I read my father's story and responded in writing, my students shared their writing with one another and me and learned from each other's stories. We created a parallel endeavor to use writing as a way of "coming to terms" and "sorting things out." More than anything, I wanted to model joy in this work. A student named Sofia said later, "I think that that was a good decision of yours to be getting us to think like that." My decision to be open seemed to give most students permission to be open as well. Sofia was one of the last students to grow comfortable with sharing her writing, as I describe in Chapter 3, but her response to my writing was positive: "It was good that you actually opened up to us, because then we were like, oh it's not just us. . . . I don't think it's bad because you're human, not because you're a teacher, you can tell people your life. It's like you're somebody too. . . . Because everybody was like *wow, wow you go through that too.*" On a similar note, Hazel expressed appreciation for other teachers at our school who were willing to share their experiences. She stated, "Because you guys are, like, open with us, you know, it's matured us in a huge way."

Students had different reactions to the content as well as the process they observed in my writing. Hazel related it to her parents' struggle with addiction, saying, "You couldn't even imagine them not being sick because all you know is them being that way." Patrick and Serenity tried to figure out connections between themselves and their families that held more compassion. Serenity explained, "I did really try to avoid getting into a relationship like that, I always told myself *I'm never gonna do that* . . . and I guess I walked right into one. Like I was so concerned about it that I didn't notice I was walking right into one. I guess I would write that I was blinded." Patrick began to look for holes in his story, as he stated, "I was trying to use my mom and my dad to examine both of their, not flaws, but things that they did that shaped me . . . and now I can see like ok well that certain thing is shaping me now."

Abraham was curious how the experiences I described in my writing shaped me as a teacher. It led to an interesting exchange:

*Abraham:* What do you think of, like, what if you never experienced anything, what if everything with your mom was fine, you had a

> good relationship with her, you never had bad times, you think
> you would've . . .
>
> *Ms. LaMay:* I wouldn't be me.
>
> *Abraham:* You wouldn't be you now, huh? You woulda been more, I
> think you woulda been more like a *teacher* teacher teacher.
>
> *Ms. LaMay:* What's a *teacher* teacher teacher?
>
> *Abraham:* Follow, like, just follow the books, and *do this do that while
> I sit at my desk* . . .

The connections that Abraham and I were able to make to each other's stories helped him see writing as a powerful way of confronting our perceptions of the world. After I shared my story, he described his writing as a way to "face it," admitting that "I didn't really figure it out until I started thinking about it, analyzing it and like writing it on paper and just like figuring it out. I was all, okay this, this is where I came from, these are my problems, and how can I fix them?"

I can, as Alan Peshkin describes, find myself "in the subjective underbrush of my own prose" (2000, p. 293). With respect for my students, I include these pieces of my story because it is important that the work I ask of them is work that I am willing and able to do. My discovery of my father's writing led to a major shift in my story and I include our photo in Figure 2.5. Since I shared my writing with the students in this book, I have researched borderline personality disorder much more deeply in a way that has transformed my story once again. My hope for my students is that they will build a repertoire of metacognitive life tools to dialogue with themselves in a similar desire to forge healthy, balanced, and whole lives, since it requires strategy to remember what hurts us.

**Figure 2.5. One of the Last Photos of My Dad and I**

## CHAPTER 3

# Writing the Personal-Academic School Gravity Connection

**Writer:** *noun.* A person. Someone who goes through experiences and feels like people should know about them.

—Patrick's Definition, 11th Grade English

**Revision:** *noun.* Me growing, as a person and as a writer.

—Maizie's Definition, 11th Grade English

Kylie Kama was a quiet student who was easy to overlook. She had an unassuming presence and was not a discipline problem. She tended to go passively along with others and show little emotion. Her real feelings were difficult to read. She had several friends, but she avoided making herself the center of attention. She rarely spoke in class and had a tendency to absent herself. Her skill at blending into the background, combined with her inconsistent work habits, placed her at risk of falling through the cracks academically if her teachers were not paying attention.

For Kylie, school gravity required a social-emotional element. Academics were a struggle for her, and she was diagnosed with a learning disability, which meant she worked with a resource specialist every day. She did not disbelieve the rhetoric that education was the key to a "successful" life, but she would not engage with assignments that she did not understand—or that she did not find directly relevant—for the sake of a grade. She went through phases where she attempted almost no work and avoided homework completely. As a result, she frequently settled for zeroes or low grades that she either ignored or scrambled to make up at the last minute.

Her life outside of school was erratic, and it was normal for her to move from home to home. Both of her parents struggled with addiction, and neither was in a stable situation. Kylie described contentious relationships with both of them. She was accustomed to sudden ruptures and reconciliations within her family. Based on her descriptions, it seemed that her mother had a pattern of involving herself in abusive relationships, which frequently exposed her children to domestic violence.

Kylie was one of the first students in the class to engage with the narratives and essays presented in this book. She turned in her first narrative on time and finished her second before it was due. This was monumental for her. Her first academic essay was the longest paper she had ever given to me, and it was her first real attempt at academic writing. Over her five pieces of writing, she continually tried to work through a complex problem that emerged from her life story and lent itself directly to academic and literary analysis.

Kylie's personal and academic writing began to inform one another in ways that were representative of many students in the class. In this chapter, I present a range of their responses to the writing tasks, and I show how different students were able to connect to the curriculum on their own terms to arrive at a blend of personal and academic writing that allowed them to grow as learners and people.

In our conversations, Kylie was clear that life lessons were a determining factor in her decision to engage with writing. She explained, "I don't like writing, like if you didn't have the life lessons, I wouldn't see the point of doing your papers, so I wouldn't do them. Because why would I want to worry about something when it's not happening in my life?"

## BLENDING GENRES: "A WRITER IS JUST A PERSON"

This chapter elucidates the interrelation between personal narrative and academic writing and the many reasons why it can be advantageous for students like Kylie to explore how personal and academic thinking can work in tandem.

It was obvious to me when I began working with my students that most of them did not intuitively understand the purpose of academic writing. They found it a strange and awkward form of communication with conventions that seemed pointless and somewhat silly. To avoid it, they would sometimes opt out of assignments or give minimum effort. It was clear that they did not perceive academic writing as a potentially helpful forum for working through issues that seemed *real* to them.

At the end of our second year together, I sat down with as many students as I could and asked them to talk to me about their writing. I wanted to know their feelings about it, and if those feelings had changed in terms of how they saw its value. I also asked them their definition of *writer* and whether they considered themselves to be a writer.

Some students described a tangible difference in their approach to writing. Serenity explained, "I used to do assignments *that day*, and I'd always put a date like way before when it's supposed to be due so it looks like I did it before. I was like *oh I'll write about it later, I'll do it later 'cause yeah it's not that important*, like I'll just keep pushing it out of my schedule to like sleep or something." Then she described how her writing had developed substance, saying, "I'm gonna put it in a way . . . I guess my words had no shadows. Now they have shadows, there's something behind them. Before, they were like freakin' pieces of string with nothing, like thin air, like they weren't even really there. And now they actually mean stuff."

Another student, Abraham, whose work is featured in Chapter 5, presented similar views. His past feelings toward writing were negative, as he explained, "Like before I was like *naw I don't wanna do this*. I wouldn't even like carrying a pencil with me." In describing how his views had changed, he noted, "I love writing now, like I face it. I feel like I can give more details and I feel like writing is a part of life. Without writing it's like I would feel clueless."

Students did not come to these realizations solely through academic writing. It was difficult for them to see the connection between personal and academic thinking until many of them attempted writing in both genres. Depending on their comfort level and inclination, all students had the option of writing only personal narrative or academic prose. Most students attempted both types of assignments, and as they blended genres, the connection between the two became more apparent. Hazel, featured in Chapter 4, was one of the first to understand this. While she was working on one of her *Song of Solomon* essays, she explained to me, "I'm having trouble with this because it's an academic paper. But I'm trying to relate to it, like the reason why I've been pushing myself to do it is because I'm trying to relate it to my personal papers, because it does relate . . . when Milkman goes to Danville, like that's where I'm at right now . . . that's where I think I'm connecting with my academic paper." Through her metaphor, Hazel was trying to develop an angle on academic writing as an opportunity to discover new philosophical ground, just as *Song of Solomon*'s main character does in the second half of the novel that she was writing about.

Theoretical backing for genre blending is abundant. John Dewey argued over a century ago that the use of language in school was "unnatural . . . not growing out of the real desire to communicate vital impressions and convictions. . . . There is all the difference in the world between having something to say and having to say something" (1900, p. 56). Dewey noted that teachers too often devised mechanisms to force artificial language that was divorced from students' realities. My 21st-century students were quick to perceive that without a real stake in a real issue, the work of writing could easily become fake.

Paulo Freire emphasizes this need for *realness* in his idea of the "word-world." He is adamant about the integrity of this approach for connecting with students like mine, insisting that pedagogy should respect and integrate their "actual language . . . anxieties, fears, demands, dreams" (1987, p. 6). The "word-world" is a genre blend of our personal and social worlds and the written words that we encounter. Freirian literacy theory suggests that each informs the other. A student named Patrick echoed this idea when he stated to our class that "you grow academically off your past experiences." His parallel of personal and academic thinking also translated to his definition of a writer. When I asked if he considered himself to be a writer, he explained, "Now I do. Actually, I've always considered myself a writer but I didn't know what a writer was in school. Now I think a writer is just a person. Someone who goes through experiences and feels like people should know about them."

I wanted my students to define *writer* as someone who has a relationship with writing, because this is a description that many of them fit. I realized that not all in their repertoire of life experience was literature-worthy, and some of their adolescent concerns could seem trivial. There is a difference, though, between self-indulgence and self-awareness. One connotes self-centeredness, and the other points to self-perception. In *The Performance of Self in Student Writing,* Thomas Newkirk (1997) argues that writing can serve a developmental need when young people grapple earnestly with questions integral to their work of self. These questions can become legitimate themes in their work. To develop identities as writers, students need to engage in writing that generates intellectual and emotional intrigue and allows them to voice perspectives at their developmental level even as they are encouraged to deepen their views.

For Kylie and other students, their connection with personal assignments gave them a real purpose and meaning for academic writing. Patrick described personal writing as work that "gives me this whole different definition of what my all of my writing should mean or how I should do it." His brother, Nate, expressed a similar view on what he termed the "personal stuff . . . after you're done most people get like a sense of direction, they feel better with themselves cause they did a paper that's all personal, that's why I like doing it. . . . It makes me want to learn all that academic shit, about the quotes and how to quote things right."

Carol Lee (1995, 2007) argues that culturally relevant instruction should begin with and build on the knowledge and understanding that students bring to school. The goal is to help students perceive how their personal and academic identities can connect. A student-centered approach can bridge curriculum with their experience and value their competencies; it can also allow them to explore the agency reflected in the practice of disciplinarians (Ladson-Billings, 1995; Lee, 2007). Opportunities to positively engage with curricula that align with a discipline can support the development of academic identity, because positive engagement ties to our human need to grow and express competence (Marks, 2000; Newmann, 1992). This nexus of competence, confidence, and engagement is fundamental to the pedagogy of writing.

To develop identities as writers, students need at least *some* opportunities to write from experience about what they genuinely understand. If we deny them these opportunities, we may sabotage what Elbow calls "the essential dynamic of writers" (1995, p. 81). Elbow pinpoints the evaluative nature of the classroom as one where students usually find themselves "writing up" to teacher authority, resulting in a common subtext in their papers that asks, "Is this okay?" (p. 81). Writers, in contrast, generally write from a higher place of authority than their readers with a subtext that claims, "Listen to me, I have something to tell you" (p. 81). A writing course should include some assignments that let students write like writers. Hybrid essays that blend personal experience with analytical framing are increasingly common in first-year composition courses for this reason. Their aim is to help students form critical perspective in a familiar mode before asking them to manipulate theoretical material (Elbow, 1991).

It is important to note that personal and academic writing are hybrids, not opposites. Multiple dimensions of the personal may appear in various permutations in an academic piece of writing. For example, any combination of the topic, the language, the thinking, or the writer's goal may be personal, and within these categories are infinite variations of personal thinking applied to non-personal topics, non-personal thinking applied to personal topics, and so on (Elbow, 1991).

Newkirk (2014) argues that elements of narrative embed in the deep structure of all written genres. He defines narrative as a "causal understanding of the world" that transfers to the causal connections we create in academic arguments (p. 19). He explains, "there is the work of demonstration, claims and evidence and analysis, and [academic] writing can fail when these are done poorly—but these exist in a macrostructure of narrative, a story of inquiry" (p. 118).

As I read my students' narratives, I observed how their causal thinking informed the arguments they embedded in their personal stories. In most cases, they created stories from life experience based on their interpretation of selected evidence, then treated their stories as evidence on which to base life decisions. Their process involved making claims about their experience, backing up these claims with analysis, and drawing conclusions that translated to beliefs they lived by.

By the end of our curriculum, Diego decided that academic writing, despite its conventions, meant more than a sell-out to arbitrary academic authority. He reasoned that academic writing was inevitably an extension of its author. He explained to me, "I wrestle with that because it's hard to write just an academic paper. You know what I mean? Like your voice is always gonna be in the paper even if what you're saying might not always be as valuable to you." Diego's reference to "voice" suggested that personal and social perspectives could translate to academic writing, even when the content did not feel directly relevant.

From a composition standpoint, "voice" embodies the human presence, character, and sensibility in our writing (Newkirk, 2014). It can also emerge in our capacity to speak or write from a conscious theoretical stance (Danielewicz, 2008). bell hooks (1994) identifies "voice" as a process of *coming to voice* through the strategic telling of one's experience, which can facilitate students' ability to speak with authority on other matters. Narrative work pushed some of my students to tell their experience with deeper strategy and sensibility, which helped them grow more conscious of the positions they held that translated to their academic voice.

## A SEQUENCE OF LOVE PAPERS

Over the course of the curriculum, students wrote three personal narratives interspersed with two academic essays, as shown in Figure 3.1. Their first task was to define love, and their second task was to attempt to tease out a *narrative template*, or internalized story, that lay underneath their definition.

A narrative template is a schematic structure or "cookie cutter plot" with potential to generate multiple stories in its likeness (Wertsch, 2008). James Wertsch developed the idea from Vygotsky's (1978) notion of *internalization*, or the "mechanisms by which internalized thought operate[s] within the functional system of the self" (Bazerman, 2004, p. 56). This concept underlies the idea of internal narratives that can develop through internalization of experience. They can become templates, or set storylines that we carry in our hearts and minds.

To help my students visualize this idea, I borrowed a collection of Christmas cookie cutters from colleagues. I brought in my rolling pin and flour, some cutting boards, and some rolls of cookie dough from the grocery. I held up different cookie cutters and told students to think of them as "templates," and I asked them to identify patterns before imprinting them on the dough. We worked our way through angels, reindeer, trees, bells, Santas, snowmen, and candy canes, and arrived at the notion that the cookie cutters could represent story patterns we carry within us that can shape the ways we read and alter experience.

Following the second narrative assignment, students attempted their first academic essay, which was an analysis of a character or character relationship that they chose from *Song of Solomon*. I asked them to read the ways their character(s) tried to give or receive love and to identify clues in their stories and story templates as to why they loved in certain ways.

The third narrative assignment—the *Why Me* Revision—was inspired by Hazel, who is featured in the next chapter. The students' task was to try to identify an experience they had written as a *why me* story, and reconceptualize its revision in a template that was broader and more complex. In Chapter 4, my students and I define the *why me* story as one that we tend to fall back on when we do not know another way to make sense of a difficult life experience. *Why me* is sometimes the only story we know how to access.

**Figure 3.1. A Sequence of Love Papers**

| (#1) Personal Narrative | What Is Love? |
|---|---|
| (#2) Personal Narrative | Draw/Write Love Narrative Template |
| (#3) Academic Essay | *SOS* Character Analysis |
| (#4) Personal Narrative | *Why Me* Narrative Revision |
| (#5) Academic Essay | *SOS* Analysis and Revision |

The problem is that it tends to displace more comprehensive understandings. The goal for students was not to delegitimize their *why me* story, but to recognize the limitations it imposed on their personal agency. I did not expect students to magically hit upon a new narrative. Life story revision is messy, long-term work. It is a process, not a task that can be achieved through one paper. I realized that if students were genuinely engaging with their stories, then they were likely to struggle with this assignment. I still wanted them to engage with the process, even if this meant that they pulled away from familiar stories and got stuck because they were not sure where to go or how to develop the revision.

I asked students on their final academic paper to think back to their earlier essay and consider if their *why me* revision led them to read the novel differently. I wanted them to return to the notion of love and to answer the question, how does *Song of Solomon* show love?

## ALISHA'S ACADEMIC STORIES

Different students engaged in unique ways with these five papers, and they built school gravity through different aspects of the curriculum. Students varied in their engagement with the literature and its historical context and characters, as well as with the narratives and academic writing, so student choice was an essential component of the curriculum's success. Yazzie-Mintz and McCormick emphasize that "students experience the same processes differently, adults do not mechanically teach and interact with every student in exactly the same way, and engagement is a complex process that does not happen the same way every time and with every person" (2012, p. 758). Some students wrote only the personal narratives, and others wrote only the academic papers. I did not want to demand student compliance in terms of their completing every piece of writing in the "right" format and the "right" order. I did not cultivate an "anything goes" approach but rather let students adjust, self-monitor, and engage with their writing as it fit their thinking in ways that worked for them. Regardless of the writing tasks they chose, many students articulated clear connections between their personal and academic thinking across their bodies of work.

On the first day that students journaled in class to the question *What is love?*, Alisha was one of two students who asked for a moment outside to manage her emotional response to the question. I looked at her paper and it read, "I don't wanna talk about it." When I spoke with her, she said, "Love is just another way to say okay I am ready to get my heart broken." She told me that she was uncomfortable with the narrative assignments, and she asked if she could write fictional stories instead. Given the narrative theme of the curriculum, I thought this was an ideal alternative. I suspected that Alisha's fictional stories would enable her to address her experiences with love in a substantive but more comfortable way. Memory researchers have built from Tomkins's (1987) script theory to show how scripts, or story schema, that appear in our memories often translate into the fictional stories that we imagine. In one study, Amy Demorest and Irving Alexander (1992) asked people to narrate defining memories and then identified the prominent interpersonal scripts. A month later, they asked the same individuals to write fictional stories, and they found a striking overlap in the scripts embedded in each individual's memories and fictional stories. Alisha described a similar overlap in our conversations about her writing.

When I asked Alisha to describe how she thought of her stories, she explained, "I write them and I base it off the things that happen in my life. Some parts are true and some parts aren't . . . I think I write like this 'cause I don't really like talking about my experience. Just drop hints in bits and pieces." When I asked if there were any themes that recurred in her stories, she replied, "I think the main theme is relationships." I asked her why, and she told me, "I don't know. I guess 'cause my past. 'Cause like I've noticed I meet new people and get hella close to them, then somehow they leave my life."

Alisha wrote all of the academic essays, and all of them centered on the theme of interpersonal relationships. She inquired into the reasons why certain characters were afraid to love, and she explored how their fears affected their family relationships. When I asked her to talk about her academic writing, she said the thinking behind it originated from her personal life. The way she put it, she had trouble writing about herself in the first person, even though her personal story bled into her academic work. She described, "Like if it's academic and I feel like I'm not making it *I* and *me*, then I can do it. The one I'm writing right now, actually I'm enjoying writing it. That's why I told you it's gonna be hard for me to end it."

Like Kylie, Alisha created school gravity through the social-emotional element of the academic curriculum. She chose to engage her personal narrative through academic reading and writing in ways similar to what Toni Morrison describes as the inroads into characters' internal lives that serve as paths into our own: "Like Frederick Douglass talking about his grandfather, or James Baldwin talking about his father . . . these people are my access to me; they are my entrance into my own interior life" (p. 115). Martha Nussbaum (1995) complements Morrison's view that literature can create a safe space for us to think about ourselves in the third person. Literary characters can encourage us to take risks and face stories that we have trouble confronting directly. Nussbaum writes, "Literary works that promote identification and emotional reaction cut through those self-protective stratagems, requiring us to see and to respond to many things that may be difficult to confront" (p. 6).

A sensitive issue Alisha explored through her academic work was her confusion around how family members should appropriately show love.

Her opening lines read:

> In the book *Song of Solomon* by Toni Morrison, Ruth Foster Dead
> tries to find love in all the wrong ways. She tries to find love with the
> men in her life. But she tries doing it in a way that love shouldn't be
> shown with family. It seems like Ruth has good reasons for what she
> does but they're not good enough. Actually for what she does there are
> no good reasons at all.

As she wrote on, she observed that key family members were missing
from certain characters' lives. Her interpretation echoed "in bits and pieces"
selective parts of her own story.

> Maybe she's like that because her mother might not have been around.
> If she wasn't, then it would have been harder for Ruth to see how
> women should show love to certain people, since it's a possibility that
> she only lived with her dad. Living with a dad can be hard to learn
> how to show love.

Alisha's academic writing probed the notion that people *learn* to show love,
which connected to the theme of her stories and her desire to understand why
she would grow close to certain people and then realize they were gone. Through
her literary analysis, she recognized that people tend to show love according to
how they learned it, even if this means avoiding love out of fear of abandonment.
As she reflected in conversation on her academic paper, she told me:

> Well I finished the part about self-love and Ruth, and I moved on to
> like family love . . . I guess it's 'cause of Macon II, I guess he's like
> scared to form a relationship after, 'cause like his mom died, and then
> he saw his dad get killed, and then he thought his sister betrayed him
> when she and the gold just disappeared out of the cave. And then
> he moved and then he met Ruth and they had two kids, and then he
> stopped sleeping with her, and then he was thinking like *oh, man,*
> *we're having kids, well if we get closer, if we get too close she's gonna*
> *hurt me or the kids are gonna leave me,* or yeah. And just the way
> Ruth thinks about how to form a relationship or try to find love in
> ways that, like it's not really there. It's there to her but it's not there to
> the other person. Her dad let her do it and she didn't have nobody else
> to tell her right from wrong.

Despite Alisha's resistance to narrative writing, she used academic writing
to engage in narrative work that she did not voice directly through the "I."
As a result, her academic work evolved some mature insights about love and
relationships as she probed deeply into personal territory.

For Alisha and many others, love became a generative topic that pushed them to surface and build on the knowledge and "actual language . . . anxieties, fears, demands, dreams" that they brought to their work (Freire, 1987, p. 6). It allowed them to self-differentiate. A student named Maizie, whose work is discussed later in this chapter, expressed how it was helpful to have options where "you don't have to write it exactly one way because you can go on and on . . . from one subject you can go all out." Love captured students' attention because it touched their emotions, but it also allowed them a range of choice in deciding how personal to be. As students wrote about the characters, they understood more and more that their ways of being came from somewhere and evolved from a context they wanted to unravel. Love kindled their desire for greater understanding and facilitated their discovery that personal awareness could be enhanced by academic work.

## NATE: MAKING A "WHOLE STORY"

Nate resisted the personal narratives for a different reason than Alisha. He initially insisted that he did not buy into the narratives because he had no story to tell. He attempted to write them, but he made it clear that he preferred academic work.

In his first narrative, he wrote, "I'm not like other people, I'm not an emotional person . . . I'm trying to be as open as I can and it's really hard because I don't have any strong personal story that affects me strong enough to have a breakthrough moment."

In his second narrative, he reiterated this sentiment with a little more detail: "We all have a certain type of story that shapes us. For me it's nothing special, it's a boring story . . . nothing interesting I have in my mind to share. I wish I could give you something like a heartfelt story but there's nothing. Yeah my father died but I always kept the same output on life. All that did for me is teach me that life is short and you could die at any moment any time. What you put out in the world is how people are going to remember you."

Nate's first academic essay focused on the fractured relationship between two main characters and former best friends, Milkman Dead and Guitar Bains. Nate located the relationship between Guitar and Milkman in an historical context. He represented them through the metaphor of oil and water, stating in his introductory paragraph that "the two ingredients will mix at first but later after letting it sit the water and oil will start to separate from each other . . . right here were two types of people who will never really become friends, but they did anyway, to become the best of buddies." Nate's metaphor and nuanced understanding of the relationship between Milkman and Guitar was in line with Toni Morrison's description of these characters as "brothers . . . two men who love each other but nevertheless have no area in which they can talk" (Taylor-Guthrie, 1994, p. 111). Nate identified Milkman and Guitar as "different people who have differences to the story that makes a whole story." This is similar to how Morrison explains it, arguing that her characters embody "certain poles, and certain kinds of thought, and certain kinds of states of being . . . struggling for sovereignty or some sort of primacy. And there are lessons in that sense" (Taylor-Guthrie, 1994, p. 178).

Nate understood more than most other students how the characters' personal stories were grounded in history. Here, he found school gravity. Instead of moving from his personal narrative to the historical, which Diego exemplifies in Chapter 5, Nate started with the historical. Nate's academic writing centered on the premise that history plays out in people's personal lives. Despite his reticence to tell his story, he intuitively understood this idea.

In Nate's second essay, he began to analyze the connections between characters' histories and personal stories that he had dismissed as nonexistent in his life. He focused on the generational succession of the Dead family men, from the original Macon Dead (Jake) to Macon II and his son Milkman (Macon III):

> Milkman's lack of love interest can be traced back to his father Macon. . . . Macon is just a hustler, a plain regular hustler. Macon's father Jake was one of the richest men in his little town in Virginia. Owning the most land for an ex-slave during a time when African-Americans didn't even have a voice is incredibly amazing. But all of that was just taken from him, murdered in front of his two children's eyes.

Nate's analysis of father-son relationships tied to the integration of historical and personal narratives that Morrison describes: "I wanted to translate the historical into the personal. I spent a long time trying to figure out what it was about slavery that made it so repugnant, so personal, so indifferent, so intimate, and yet so public . . . the kind of information you can find between the lines of history. It's right there in the intersection where an institution becomes personal, where the historical becomes people with names" (Denard, 2008, pp. 76–77). Through his academic writing, Nate managed to translate the historical into the personal in a way that emerged in his last personal narrative, which he turned in *after* his final academic essay, in the order that worked for him.

He opened his narrative with a father-son comparison that conveyed the intergenerational theme of his story.

> Me and my father we are pretty much the same. I could already tell that I'm going to be just like him. . . . That's where my meaning of love comes into place. Somebody told me I had the most positive negative attitude in life. . . . That's how I was raised man, cause my father told me *the only thing that matters in life is to make money and support your family.* That's my motto. . . . That's what he did, that's his

grandpa before him and his dad before that, that's where I come from, a family like that.

I have the thought of *all the men in my family die young,* so I got my uncle right now, and he's so sick, and right now I think he's on an urge to die in the next two or three years . . . and my grandpa, he died young, and my dad, he died at 36. My uncle Jason, he died in San Quentin at the age of 28, murdered. So . . . all this stuff in my family, I have it in my head that I'm gonna die young. It's not the quantity or how long you live, it's the quality that you pull out, so that's what I'm trying to do, so . . . I'm kinda hoping I make it to 40.

I think of Macon the second. Watching his father die at a young age made him want material things that didn't die, and me, I'm trying to get as much material possessions as I could before I die, I don't care what it takes, I'm gonna make me some money . . . I'm also the third in the family. Milkman you know he's living his life, you know, he doesn't really care about anything. Sometimes, I follow in that path, I just don't really care, you wanna just go through life and pretty much that's it.

I asked Nate if he felt he had grown as a writer from any of the work he had done. He explained, "I can say that this year is the first time of me ever writing anything . . . I've grown to respect my work a little more, cause before I'd just write the shit without even thinking, most of the time copy off other kids, I'd just like turn it in just to make the grade. But now I wanna take more feelings in my work now . . . I like writing essays more now."

When I asked if he had grown as a person, his answer was dicier: "For me, I will always find happiness in a piece of shit. Maybe because I think I might live a short life."

## SOFIA AND MAIZIE: "GIVING SOMETHING BACK THAT'S REAL"

Throughout the curriculum, one of my goals was for students' writings on love to merge with the discourse of school to create a type of "third space." Kris Gutiérrez, Betsy Rymes, and Joanne Larson (1995) identify traditional classroom roles and discourses as teacher "scripts" and student "counterscripts." The third space is a "transitional, less rigidly scripted space" where a genuine merging of teacher and student views and voices can occur (p. 452). When the teacher alone defines what counts as legitimate knowledge, then dialogue amounts to students entering the teacher's script on the teacher's terms. In a truer dialogic pedagogy, "students . . . have opportunities to elaborate on and incorporate their own narratives into the larger classroom text" (p. 452).

Students brought their own definitions of love—they *had* to—to serve as primary texts for the foundation of their work. I could not tell them what love meant to them. Nor could I qualify how they experienced it. I could not identify specific themes and events in their unwritten stories or dictate how their revisions should take shape. To a large extent, students had to be the experts. This meant deciding what mattered enough to address and using their judgment to determine their process.

Sofia was one student whose selective engagement with the curriculum intrigued me. She did not turn in a single piece of take-home writing during her first 18 months in my class. Contrary to Nate and Alisha, Sofia worked persistently to complete all three personal narratives during her fourth semester. She turned them in on her own time frame when she decided they were "done," including the *why me* revision, which was almost a month late and 15 pages long.

Despite my pleading, she did not engage with the academic writing.

She did read *Song of Solomon* and asked to take the book home and read ahead. This was the first independent reading I had seen her do. She reminded me of this at the end of the year, recalling, "Yeah, remember you would just put books there and before I would be like *naw I don't wanna read this, it's too long*, and when you showed us the *Song of Solomon* one, like when we started going through all the writing of *Song of Solomon* I was like *oh my God I actually want to read this book* and that's why I asked you for the book, I was like *can I take it home* and you were like *yeah sure*. Yeah and I started reading it."

Even though Sofia declined to do the academic writing, she did a lot of academic thinking over the curriculum. She explained to me, "Well before I didn't really see myself doing the academics or the reading because I didn't really think I could do it, and now . . . I feel more free to be able to do something like that." She used characters from the reading to challenge her personal tendencies, as she revealed, "I actually had like a whole fucking week of me fighting myself about Ruth." When I asked her to describe this "fight," she told me, "'Cause you remember I was like *oh my mom my mom my mom*, she reminds me so much about my mom. And it's not just her, it's me too, I was like *see that thing about Ruth*, or *most things about Ruth*, it was me too, like me blaming others about what I have done. Or what I'm doing. And it was like *ugh*, yeah."

Sofia was not comfortable opening up to people who were not in her inner circle. This had played out in a painful way for us the year before. I had asked students to journal on a prompt about a time when they felt invisible. Sofia had written a full page and a half by the time I walked by her desk, and I stopped to read over her shoulder. I whispered that I appreciated her answer and responded to a few lines she had shared. She shut down and stopped speaking to me. We ended up in the dean's office as he tried to mitigate the conflict. She told me that I had not had her permission to say anything about her writing loudly enough for anyone around her to hear. She was right. I apologized, but by the end of year she was barely speaking to me.

Sofia's choice to engage with the narratives indicated a change from her previous discomfort with being vulnerable. She identified this anxiety at the center of her love template.

> I've been so sad for so long . . . I never let myself be loved. I pushed everyone away. And still today I push them away because it's in the back of my head I always have that doubt of if they really love me or if it's just a front. That's why I always act like I don't care. And I know when it's like that I won't talk to that person or hang out with them. I have to really feel like their love is real for me so I can really put myself out there for that person or persons.

Sofia expressed that her wanting to get past her fear of "putting herself out there" was the main reason she wrote the narratives. She relayed to me some of her self-dialogue: "Yeah 'cause I was like *if I don't do this, I'm never gonna feel free to be like, to tell somebody I don't really know or who doesn't really know me something about me.* Yeah 'cause remember before I would be like *nooo, get away.*" Conversations with Sofia sometimes included her closest friend, Maizie, who was one of very few students she trusted. Even so, Sofia disclosed that Maizie had been the first to make the effort. She described, "I didn't want nobody to get too close to me. I only allowed her because she opened up to me and I felt like I needed somebody there. I was new at school and I didn't know nobody there. I was like *I like her.* . . . So I was like, whatever, she's an exception."

Like Sofia, Maizie turned in all of the narratives. She also tried the academic writing even though she did not like it. Similar to Kylie in the beginning of the chapter, Sofia and Maizie emphasized that the personal writing was what drew their interest in school because it pushed them to be honest. Maizie explained, "I didn't really see your essays as homework. I just see it as me being real. And just like letting somebody know what I have to tell. I think you were looking for not lying, like actually giving something back that's real, and that would be our grade, or not a grade but that would be your thank you. You know?" I asked if grades played a role in their decision to do the writing, and they both said no. Honesty proved to be a key factor in creating school gravity for them instead.

At the end of year, Sofia and Maizie conveyed their views on school and writing, and how they had changed over the semester. The change was in their sense of growth as learners and people. Maizie emphasized learning as meaningful when "it shows us something about us and something about school . . . if you're gonna go to college and stuff like that you need to learn about yourself too." Her process of confronting herself made the narratives difficult to write, but it also made her more determined to finish. She explained, "Yes it was hard to write it. I was like, *how should I say it, should I say it like this*, 'cause the last paper, it was freaking hard . . . but I knew what I wanted to say. . . . Do you know how many days I spent at least trying to write a little bit? Since the day you gave it, I was like *maaaannn, how am I gonna write this?*"

Sofia and Maizie felt that they grew as writers in part because they had considerable control over their writing process. Andrea Lunsford (2007) emphasizes that students and teachers alike may struggle to revamp traditional authority structures that are deeply ingrained in our sense of what a classroom is. Yet a classroom can be a hard place for students to negotiate writers' identities if the class structure does not allow them some autonomy. The culture of writing can clash with the culture of schools, but an effective writing classroom must sometimes deviate from a larger educational system that does not address how different students learn or why they engage and instead measures achievement via easily quantifiable outputs. The human factor that distinguishes a classroom from an assembly line caused our class process to evolve into many individualized writing processes and products. In the end, this was a good thing.

Since my students ran with the assignments in quite different ways, it was important that their processes drove their outcomes rather than the other way around. Alisha wrote fictional stories that led to academic essays, while Thomas wrote academic essays that led to narrative perceptions and Sofia wrote narratives that led her to realize why "it's not always bad to open up and just be real." Their difference in process shaped how they approached the actual writing. For example, Maizie felt that foresight mattered in her writing to the point where she explained, "Okay you're gonna think about it and you're gonna be like *I'm gonna do this right*." Meanwhile, Nate insisted that "most of the time when I write a paper, I write with as much of a blank mind as I could, 'cause if I write it with a blank mind, it helps me grow out."

Sofia and Maizie were determined to grow through their work, which meant writing and rewriting as they needed to. In doing so, they took on revision without realizing it. This partly explained their habit of turning in their papers late. If I had returned their papers and told them to rewrite, they would likely have rejected the request, but unprompted and left to their own devices, they were both willing to work through multiple narratives and push their thinking on the same hard issues each time. Maizie described, "Well to me it didn't really feel that I was writing about the same thing. It was me growing, as a person and as a writer. In the last paper I felt like I basically talk about the same thing kind of like in my past paper. . . . I could be *oh well I talked about it before*, but this one was like more, I was trying to make it more like clear. I was trying so hard to be so specific, but I was having trouble with it still a little bit."

Both girls, pictured in Figure 3.2, described a change in their perception of writing and its importance. They defined "good writing" as real language with real associations. Maizie voiced a strong view on this point:

I think good writing to some people is a lot about trying to use big words or trying to make it sound very professional, very Stanford. But it's just making it real, just being real with yourself. A language where people are like *damn this is real, this is real, this is real*. I think that's

**Figure 3.2. Sofia and Maizie on Twin Day**

good writing right there, 'cause that's a book I would wanna read, you know, something real. Not something that's all proof with very big words. There's always those papers that have to be very academic, but that's so hard.

I think writing should be connected to life. It should be about life, that's what writing is. If it was gonna help you in life and it's something that you love to do, then why couldn't it be something, at least make it something, I mean, it could be anything but as long as it's real. There's always something that connects to you. If you love writing, somehow some way it connects to you. And that's what makes it good and makes people wanna read it.

While the personal writing felt the most valuable to Maizie, she also acknowledged some academic takeaways and the sense that personal and academic thinking could relate to make education matter. Maizie emphasized that, to her, the personal *was* academic because learning was essentially about developing insight. She explained, "I think when I have homework assignments I'll probably look at them like *you know I don't like academics, but you have to do it,* but what really basically gets us is the personal and just being real. Like what you have and your opinion, I think that's educational. That's you. Even if it's your opinion, you're still learning, you're still opening up, you're using your head, using your brain, your brain is growing by thinking and just spitting things out. Even if they're not big words."

## KYLIE'S NARRATIVE "LIMBO" AND OTHER THEMES

Several students in the class attempted all five pieces of writing in the arrangement laid out earlier in the chapter. A pattern of intertextuality emerged in their set of five papers that was illustrative of Newkirk's point that our argument positions often result from "hard and important narrative work" (2014, p. 116).

Students' love narratives pushed them to articulate positions they held on life issues that extended into their interpretations of academic text. The narrative templates that emerged in their personal writing also influenced how they framed academic arguments. Conversely, some of the moves they made as academic thinkers and writers influenced how they saw themselves as people. Their essays helped many of them pinpoint problem spots or contradictions in their stories that they tried to work out in their *why me* revisions. Revisions in one genre usually led to revisions in the other.

Narrative themes frequently developed from the personal questions that arose in their love narratives and guided their thinking over the next several papers. Examples of these themes are shown in Figure 3.3.

**Figure 3.3. Love Narrative Themes**

| Case Student | Personal Narrative Theme | *Song of Solomon* Essay Focus |
|---|---|---|
| Abraham | Dealing with hard truths and self-legitimacy | Truth and self-legitimacy in Guitar's story |
| Hazel | Shifting from *why me* → *why them* in analysis of her parent–child relationships | Parent–child relationships between Macon II and Ruth Dead and their three children |
| Kylie | "Victim stories," addiction, and a state of narrative limbo | The perpetuation of unhealthy personal relationships—Milkman and Hagar |
| Diego | A life theme of struggle—do we shape our stories or do our stories shape us? | The conversion of one's story into positive or negative energy in Guitar and Malcolm X |
| Nate | Intergenerational story of men in his family who die young | The historical legacy of the Dead family men |
| Alisha | Love and loss in personal and family relationships | Learning to show love and overcome fear of loss in Dead family relationships |

Kylie Kama, whose words open this chapter, combined her personal and academic writing in a way that facilitated her growth in both genres. As she developed a deeper understanding of her personal story, her academic writing developed more depth. Kylie focused her narrative work on the problem of unhealthy personal relationships. When I asked why this issue mattered to her, she offered some background on her family that took me a minute to follow. Her convoluted explanation below was evidence of the emotional confusion that she would use her writing as a tool for sorting through.

> Long story . . . because my sister's dad and my mom are together but her mom . . . okay wait, let me see if I can do this. Okay her uncle married a Samoan lady, which is my auntie by marriage. And then my auntie by marriage has a brother, and he has a Mexican wife. And but they're not together any more. And then my mom got with my sister, well my stepsister's dad. Do you understand that? So like now my sister's mom doesn't like my mom 'cause she got with her husband. So now my mom's having a baby by her husband, she has like three weeks left and I found out on my birthday. I was just like *nooo*.

Kylie's first narrative turned on her belief that love was a fantasy and did not exist. She defined love as a kind of addiction with irreconcilable drama. Her second narrative sketched a pattern in which love inevitably led to pain because it was impossible to create on equal terms. She described relationships as situations where one person took control and the other hoped for mercy or kindness. Kylie's first read of *Song of Solomon* was that this exact situation happened to Hagar. Her first essay analyzed Milkman as a careless, "lost soul" whose actions were reprehensible, and Hagar as a "crazy woman" who could not handle rejection. As Kylie grew to better understand the role that she played in her own story, she began to see both of these characters differently.

Kylie's third personal narrative marked an important shift in the progression of her story. She came to the realization that imbalanced relationships were not inevitable or fated, but were sometimes the result of what she termed a "victim story." She defined this story as one that she developed when she felt victimized by society or someone she loved, yet powerless to change things. This story, she decided, was part of the addiction cycle. It also kept her in what she called a "dark place." She described, "I felt like a powerless person, feeling sorry for myself but not doing anything about it. It's like I was giving up on myself as useless."

Once Kylie identified this template in her personal story as one that underlay her first three pieces of writing, she tried to revise it, but she had trouble finding a storyline to replace it. This put her in an awkward state of mind that she called "limbo." She explained, "I'm really trying to change my 'victim story' into no story. Changing my ways of how I see everything and not sounding like I'm on replay . . . I'm starting to see some things a little

**Figure 3.4. (From Left to Right) Victoria, Serenity, Hazel, Kylie, Alisha, Kaliyah, and Dalia on the Roof of Stanford After Sharing Our Work with Credential Candidates**

differently, but at some points they come back to a limbo position. I try so hard not to go back." Kylie worked on her *why me* revision until she was literally stuck, and then turned in her paper. She did not resolve the tension in her story, but her ability to locate a problem in how she "wrote" herself helped her reframe her understanding of the relationship between Milkman and Hagar. In her second essay, she argued that Milkman learned to change his victim story by spending time in the limbo that she described. His ability to work his way out of limbo paralleled his learning to understand people instead of judge them. Her analysis of Hagar's breakdown was also different. She argued that Milkman, after much confusion, was able to begin a new story. Hagar was not, and her death showed how internalized victimization could play out in relationships in a particularly injurious way.

When Kylie reflected with me on her writing, she spoke more on her point about learning to understand people instead of judge them. She saw this as a change factor in Milkman's relationships, and she was trying to apply this lesson to herself. She explained, "Right now I'm working on my relationships with people. So I'm trying to see people in a better, like deeper way, instead of just judging them. 'Cause usually I'd just be like *eeew I don't like you*. And I wouldn't talk to you and I'd just mug you. But now after I read the book like I really just wanna know people's background." Another personal takeaway from her academic work was that she began to understand what it meant to work on herself. She explained, "Honestly now I'm starting to not really care about the drama anymore. I'm trying to like concentrate on me, like it sounds kind of selfish, but I haven't been working on myself before. So now it's coming to a point where I really have to care about me or I'm not gonna become nothing in life."

Over the course of her five papers, Kylie realized that life did not have to be a story of defeat. She wanted to write a new story, but she was not sure what it was.

It was a rhetorical beginning from a student who once stated squarely, "I would never do your papers."

## CHAPTER 4

# Revising *Why Me*

**Milkman moment:** *noun.* An epiphany; a narrative shift from why me to a broader framework that generates new understandings and possibilities; a linguistic move from the language of what one does or does not deserve to a more deeply contextualized, depersonalized articulation of one's personal and social world.

—Working Definition, 11th Grade English

Hazel initially struck me as an honest thief. Before we grew to know each other as teacher and student, her previous teachers told me stories from her 9th-grade year, when she gained notoriety in a scandal that involved stealing other students' iPods. One day during my prep, I was walking to the office and I heard someone about 50 paces behind me yell, "Mizzz LaMaaayyy!" I turned to see Hazel running toward me, holding in her hand a crumpled, folded paper. As I waited for her to catch up to me, she hollered, "Ms. LaMay. I have my homework. I know it's late, but I still want to give it to you." She followed me to the office as far as her next class took her. She talked the whole way and asked if she could come at lunch and talk some more.

My principal observed the hallway encounter and asked me afterwards if I knew about Hazel's history of running away. I did not. I learned that in her 9th-grade year, after the iPod incident, she had disappeared, and no one had known where she was for months. Another teacher at our school had finally tracked her down. From the conversation, I learned that both of her parents struggled with addiction, and she had a history of moving from one family member to another.

My principal also told me that Hazel was a writer who had stirred the audience when she performed her poetry at the school's Showcase talent show the year before. Her talent as a writer was what I was about to witness.

I was alone in my room when Hazel burst through the door halfway into the lunch period. She asked if it was okay if she read me a poem that she had written. With no idea of what I was about to hear, I agreed to be an audience. She told me that the title of her poem was "Home," and then she began to read[1]:

My mind is twisting and turning fighting at war with itself
Iraqi Korean.
Colt 45 take out the pistol, hold held bomb
You must restrain—to put the poison in my ear –
Bullet oil leak inside my brain.
Right hand—I can do this, I am who I am
I am strong I am a woman.
Left hand—I won't do this I'm not who you think I am
I'm not so strong I'm not independent.
Daddy take care of me, don't sink to that level
Shoot me back to my mom's when five years ago she was shooting up
    in her arm
Taking a little vacation, took up the pcp with no hesitation
She'd raise her hand to her head then
Swing it back to my face . . . felt like a ball getting swung by a bat.
So no running out the door going to my friends house to see my old
    cat . . .
But as I walked back, Hazel, look up at the sky,
Stars shining bright. Damn it's night.
Walking back slowly I see all the white gates seem to be locked
    but one.
Knock knock knock.
The sound of my footsteps stop.
White man nearly age 40.
White grey hair green blue eyes.
White ripped shirt he brings me on by
Covers my mouth with his nasty ass hand,
Now having me disgusted by this shit stained man.
Turning up the Indiana Jones
So now here's me crying in this world,
He yanks on the shirt of an 8 year old girl,
Not caring that I cannot breathe for
You lay your body on top of mine,
I look up asking God what the fuck is this kind of sign.
I lay my hand back I search and pull it forward.
One rock to the head does it safely.
I guess some things were good that mama taught me.
Running back home, I open the door
Mama asks where'd you go you little whore.
I try to explain the painful game, one insane man played on me.
She raises her hand, I close my eyes
I feel a drip drip drip off my face
Nice and gently she seems satisfied.
Touching my face as my skin becomes liquefied.

I asked why do you think you could put your hands on us
And do the shit you do.
She says I hit you, because I love you.
I guess it's different now, she's clean and sober, life's all fair.
But fuck all that
My memories
Have gone nowhere.
Play by play scene by scene
Blood by blood play by play
Like the words I said five seconds ago
My memories have gone nowhere.
So pops why do you think sending me away will do?
I know thoughts of wonder will be inside of you.
As I take my first puff of the secret drug.
As I take my first pcp tugging at my life.
Now you see the tears which resemble the years
Shirts get tighter, skirts get shorter, makeup gets thicker, lingerie gets
    thinner.
Now I wait for the day you raise your hand, wipe my tears, and stop
    my mind
From this fucked up Rome.
Hold me in your arms and say . . .
Welcome home.

Hazel punctuated her language with charged pauses and clear enunciation. She read with feeling and poise. When she finished, she looked at me and asked me what I thought of it. I sat stunned by the intense, raw quality of her delivery, and the degree of vulnerability she had just shown.

She did not seem to anticipate this reaction. Instead, she acted like an unassuming student who had just reached out to a teacher she hoped she could trust. She said she wanted to get to know me, and she asked if we could talk more later. Just like that, she managed to instigate a relationship with me in the space of one day.

## RUNNING, WRITING, AND SEEKING THE STORY
## BENEATH THE STORY

For Hazel, writing was more than a school gravity factor. It was her survival tool. She wrote almost every day. She wrote poetry, letters, stories, and lyrics that one of our teachers helped her put to music. As I discovered, it was characteristic for Hazel to carry around her composition book and ask others to listen as she read out loud. In this way, she was one of several students who authenticated a culture of poetry and spoken word at our school.

The summer before her senior year, she and her friend Serenity auditioned and were accepted onto their city team that competed in the Brave New Voices National Youth Poetry Slam. She had the opportunity to spend several weeks attending poetry workshops, meeting with local social activists, including Bobby Seale, cofounder of the Black Panther Party, and living in the dorms on a University of California campus. Her team made it to the semifinals of the competition. When they returned home, they were invited to meet the music group The Black Eyed Peas, who were holding an event in El Cuento to celebrate their opening of a local music academy for youth.

Hazel transformed our class dynamic more than any other student. She was a natural leader who loved to speak and perform. Her engagement brought school gravity to the ongoing work of the curriculum and kept it from losing momentum. Despite the trauma in her life, she was vibrant and engaged on most days. She was willing to say things that other students were too apprehensive to share. She did not worry about how her classmates perceived her, and in this way, she earned their respect. Her willingness to share her writing brought school gravity to the process. Whether her work was personal or academic, poetry or prose, her desire to share it was fundamental to my effort to build a community of writers who were willing to engage with one another's texts. Students learned from reading Hazel's work. The spectacular emotional effort that she put into her writing inspired others to try assignments that they might otherwise have sidestepped. She did not always turn in her work on time, but she almost always turned in every assignment.

Hazel's classmates elected her senior class president at the end of her junior year. In one of our conversations, she reflected on how students and teachers had changed their perceptions of her. Before, she was the freshman who stole iPods. Two years later, she was the new student leader of the school. She owed this transformation, in large part, to her writing.

*        *        *        *

For the past 30 years, James Pennebaker and his colleagues have studied the physiological and mental health benefits of writing. Pennebaker and Seagal explain, "Extensive research has revealed that when people put their emotional upheavals into words, their physical and mental health improves markedly" (1999, p. 1244). In a cumulative review of this work, he and R. Sherlock Campbell report that "emotional writing can influence frequency of physician visits, immune function, stress hormones, blood pressure, and a host of social, academic, and cognitive variables" (2003, p. 60). Chad Burton and Laura King (2004) show that the therapeutic benefits of writing include the narration of intensely affirmative or positive events. Their research demonstrates that the facilitation of physical and emotional health stems less from the emotional tone of the writing and more from the insight we gain into our understanding of what our emotional reactions mean.

Hazel's inclination to put her "emotional upheavals into words," as Pennebaker relates, was apparent. She was an unusual case, in that she was already using writing as a creative outlet to explore her life and traumas before I met her. Even so, she grew as a writer through our class as she learned to connect her creative writing to academic work, and as she shifted her narrative to include a range of possibilities to explain *why* certain things in her life had occurred.

Pennebaker and Seagal (1999) link our development of a healthy emotional life to the causal relationships we create as we narrate. When I met Hazel, she was overwhelmed by negative life variables and attributed them to something symptomatic about *her*.

Newkirk argues that "when we employ narrative—and approach experience as *caused* and comprehensible—we gain a measure of control. We take a stand against randomness and fatalism in favor of a world that makes sense" (2014, p. 34). What changed over the semester was Hazel's understanding of the causal relationships in her story, the larger contexts at play, and the reasons why these were not always personal. She also grew more compassionate toward herself. She reflected on her first love narrative in a conversation with me, admitting that "this paper made me notice I didn't love myself." When she pointed to her narrative template, she added, "and this one helped me see why."

Hazel tried to stabilize her emotions and her grades over the spring of her junior year, although her pattern of running away did not cease. When her anxiety escalated, her instinct was to run, but her disappearances became less drastic. Earlier in her high school career, she went missing for considerable periods of time, but by the 11th grade she made a point to maintain contact with adults at school. There was a day when she left campus mid-morning, walked several blocks to the nearby Walgreens, and then called and asked me to pick her up. One evening she got on the bus with her writing journal, rode it for a while, and then got off and wrote alone for a while before she decided to go back home. She talked to her teachers about it later:

> In the last six months, hm, six months ago I would've ran without hesitation. And then recently I did run, it was about two weeks ago, I just left. I took a bag of clothes, it was just [my ex-boyfriend] and my dad, and just things were starting to get serious with [my boyfriend], and I left, and I ran. And I just went on this bus, I didn't know where it was going. I got off in the middle of nowhere and I literally sat there and I wrote. I think I threw the paper away after but I wrote like five pages, of just writing. I was just letting everything out and then I think I buried it or something. And it was just me, me running. And last night I wrote a piece where I was like *I know running's not the solution so I'm just gonna freeze.*

Hazel was the first student to realize that changing her pattern meant changing the story beneath the story. This, we learned, was the work of narrative revision.

## NARRATIVE REVISION AND STORIES OF TRAUMA

Many students think of revision as a chore. Most of my students preferred to avoid it. Despite my numerous lectures that "good writers" do not magically write with brilliance, but commit to constant improvement, I struggled at every turn to get my students to revise their work.

So to lend school gravity to the idea of revision, I pushed my students to think of it as a potentially radical concept—not as the seemingly sterile act of fixing grammatical errors but as a more compelling, intimate process of reframing the stories we live by. We drew from Paulo Freire's description of revision as a form of praxis, whereby we can learn to increase our perceptual capacity and act creatively on the world to engage in a "certain form of *writing* it or *rewriting* it, that is, of transforming it by means of conscious, practical work" (1987, p. 10). Adrienne Rich (1979) defines revision similarly as "looking back . . . seeing with fresh eyes . . . entering an old text from a critical direction" (p. 35). Susan Florio-Ruane (1997) refers to "reemplotment," or a turn from a colonial narrative to one that relocates agency in cultural identity. In either case, the notion of revision transcends writing to encompass critical or transformative engagement with life experience.

The concept of a narrative template was important to this work. As I defined in the previous chapters, a narrative template is a schematic structure that develops as an internalized story and holds creative power to lead to repeat experiences (Wertsch, 2008). While it was obvious to students that something in their story could be different, they were not always sure what this was. Then we realized that it was necessary to locate and examine a story's deeper structure in order to change it.

In Hazel's narrative template assignment—the second in the progression of papers—she began to distill repeat experiences into a perceptible causal pattern that connected her family and personal relationships. Her writing in her love template was characteristic of her candor, as she laid out what she perceived as her personal pattern: "My love template is leaving a place or person after about two years. Ever since I can remember I've moved out of wherever I was living after two or three years. Whether I had the choice to or not. I think I get anxious when it comes to being somewhere too long. This has followed me into about three of my relationships." Hazel linked her impulse to run away to recurrent discontinuity, as she explained, "I remember in seventh grade my dad told me we were moving. . . . Ever since then I've ran away several times after I feel stationed for too long."

By the time I met Hazel, she had experienced several of the stressors identified as "adverse childhood experiences" by Vincent Felitti, Robert Anda, and other authors of the Adverse Childhood Experiences (ACE) Study (1998). When she was a student at Escenario, I was aware that she moved multiple times. She moved from her father's apartment to her grandmother's home to her mother's apartment (in a city two hours away) and back to her father's new apartment (several months later), to a room in her boyfriend's mother's home, until Child Protective Services intervened and she moved in with her aunt. Hazel's narrative template essentially outlined her trauma response.

Post-traumatic stress shows up in our schools every day in behaviors that may not appear to make rational sense, but most preparation programs do not coach educators on how to recognize and address trauma in classrooms and schools. Bruce Perry and Maia Szalavitz, authors of *Born to Love* (2014) and *The Boy Who Was Raised as a Dog—What Traumatized Children Can Teach Us About Loss, Love, and Healing* (2006), emphasize that many who work in social or public service have minimal education about trauma symptoms or the impact of trauma on children's social-emotional and cognitive development. Jeff Duncan-Andrade, a professor of education who opened Roses in Concrete, an elementary school in East Oakland, California, argues that most schools fail to provide adequate resources for addressing the social-emotional needs of students in high-trauma communities. Duncan-Andrade argues that schools and districts that *do* address trauma are barely "scratching the surface of the conversation . . . the level of investment we would need to make in case workers and mental health counselors is much more significant than just staffing up one position per school. We know what to do and have clear evidence of what to do, but we don't see it in the communities where we need it the most" (Erbentraut, 2015).

Epidemiological studies of children in urban areas show that they are frequently exposed to *complex traumas*, or multiple simultaneous and sequential stress factors. These stressors can include poverty, community violence, immigration status, family deportation, incarceration, and oppressive policing. The pervasiveness of trauma in my students' lives was not evidence of pathology in their families or communities. Rather, it was the palpable result of intergenerational and systemic oppression that debilitates communities like El Cuento and impacts the well-being of families and children. Scholarship on post-colonial stress disorder (Brave Heart & Deschenie, 2006) and post-traumatic slave syndrome (Degruy, 2005) examines the intergenerational impact of history on communities that have historically been traumatized through oppression. Dr. Kerry Ressler, who led the Grady Trauma Project, makes the case that "the rates of PTSD we see are as high or higher than Iraq, Afghanistan, or Vietnam veterans" (Propublica, 2014). Furthermore, Duncan-Andrade maintains that children who re-experience trauma may develop PTSD in ways that current research does not explain or deconstruct. He explains, "In 2011, Harvard released a new diagnosis, CPTSD, or Complex PTSD. What they're seeing happening in children's brains and bodies because of the reoccurring toxic stress [in their lives] is more complex than what we see in soldiers. So a puzzle we can't put together in soldiers has thousands more pieces for children. What we find is that [this diagnosis] explains so much in what we have been mislabeling ADHD, ADD, and misbehavior" (Independent Media Institute, 2015).

The prevalence of complex trauma can lead to *chronic toxic stress*, defined by Nadine Burke Harris as prolonged activation of the body's stress response system, which can change the developing architecture and function of the brain and organ systems. Chronic toxic stress causes the brain's amygdala to overactivate and produce continuous emergency hormones. Hazel's stress response system was constantly propelled to high alert, ready for fight or flight. Her pattern of running was primarily a flight response. She described it in her narrative template as an eruption of internal conflict, whereby her impulse to bolt would hijack her longing to stay: "I guess I do have a majority control on leaving but there is the internal war I have with myself on wanting to stay. It's happened to me so many times it's been almost a ritual . . . a cycle. A cycle impulsively."

As Hazel drew parallels in her writing between the predictable insecurity of her life and her impulse to run from intimacy or relationships—including her relationship with school—she came to an important realization: Her defense to instability was often what re-created it. Stability made her anxious, so she would collapse it in anticipation of tumult. Perry and Szalavitz explain this phenomenon in their research: "Attempting to take control of what [children] believe is the inevitable return of chaos, they appear to 'provoke' it in order to make things feel more comfortable and predictable. . . . Like everyone else, they feel more comfortable with what is 'familiar'" (2006, p. 55). This impulse to maintain familiarity was at the core of Hazel's narrative template. She presented it as a narrative and an illustrated storyboard (Figure 4.1). Her storyboard depicted in seven stages what Burke (1953) terms a "method of adjustment," which became her "manner of experiencing" (p. 152). On the left side, she showed how the pattern took shape within her family story. On the right side, she showed how the pattern played out in her personal relationships. The seven stages were:

1. Get to know
2. Get comfy
3. Accidental problems sometimes on purpose
4. Pulled away/abandoned
5. On the new search
6. Connect with new person
7. Repeat stages 1–6.

Her narrative template ended with the capitalized words, "OVER AND OVER AGAIN." Many young people like Hazel develop brilliant mechanisms for coping and surviving difficult life circumstances. When these ways of

## Figure 4.1. Hazel's Love Narrative Template

FAMILY ←————————→ RELATIONSHIPS

### 1. GET TO KNOW

Move in.                                        Find love.

### 2. GET COMFY

Stay for a while.                          Stay for a while.

### 3. ACCIDENTAL PROBLEMS SOMETIMES ON PURPOSE

Some sort of problems happen.        Find/search for problems.

### 4. PULLED AWAY/ABANDONED

Move out.                                      Stray away.

### 5. ON THE NEW SEARCH

Search for new house.                     On the hunt.

### 6. CONNECT WITH NEW PERSON

Start over again.                            Lost and found.

### 7. REPEAT 1–6

Revolving door.                             Revolving door.

coping translate to ways of being in all circumstances, however, they can be maladaptive. They can also replicate the trauma. The paradox, and a cause of the perpetual pain of Hazel's pattern, were that the strategies she employed to avoid rejection were precisely what created its repetition. In her narrative writing, she explained, "I think I try to take control of every relationship because I'm afraid to open back up to only lose them. However, in the end, I always seem to realize that *I'm the reason they're gone*. I've pushed them away by not opening up enough. Therefore that leads up to my big fear of rejection. . . . I take control only to trick myself into thinking I didn't get rejected." In turn, the sense of rejection validated her story and her fear "to not feel wanted. With my family (both sides) I don't feel wanted, so much I want to shut them out."

## THE "WHY ME" STORY

Hazel's narratives focused on self-love in the context of stressful circumstances. She identified self-love as her antidote and also recognized it as a particularly tough task for her. She wrote, "People say you gain your first love from family. However my family hasn't really shown me that unconditional, continuous love. I notice they choose to come in and out of my life whenever they please to, but I still call them my dysfunctional perfection." As a partial result, she noted some of her actions as evidence of that fact that "I had a confusing relationship with me." She explained:

> To me loving yourself is respecting yourself. It took me awhile to learn that. It was hard to understand what it meant to me to love myself. . . . I didn't care how I looked or what people thought of me when I went around punching and stealing things from people. I knew I didn't love myself but I never wanted to admit it. Since I never wanted to admit it, I made sure I wouldn't think of it. Sort of like hypnotizing myself into thinking and pretending I did.

Self-love easily got lost in Hazel's story, buried under the belief that she was the source of some of her negative experience. She also saw that self-love required revision of this narrative.

One afternoon after school, I walked into my room to see the multi-colored brainstorm in Figure 4.2 stretched across my entire board. Hazel had used every dry erase marker to turn my wall into what looked like a life-sized spoken word poem. On the left side of the board, she had written in large capital letters and boxed in the words "WHY ME." She had surrounded "WHY ME" with questions and images, bits of memory, and fragments of past conversations.

**Figure 4.2. The "Why Me" Story**

Of the isolated images and memories that appeared, one expressed, *my sister seen his crack pipe,* while another simply read *meth head.* Some of her questions were about herself, and some were about her family. One question read, *Why am I so scared?* Others asked, *What did I do to deserve this?* and *Is this where my commitment problems come from?*

Some questions wrestled with contrasting reactions and feelings: *Why do they enjoy my pain? Will I ever be able to truly stand up to them or will I always be hypnotized in their fucked up shadows?*

Other questions were followed by possible answers. Under the question *Why doesn't he/she truly love me as their kid?* she had written, *Some people don't know how to react, they've never learned. They did learn bad habits from someone (their parents) and they are so used to the easy give-up lifestyle.*

Under her own prompt, *Why did I do wrong as a kid? It's all my fault. I acted out to get some attention bcuz it wasn't given to me how I wanted. The answer lies partially in between kid + parent.*

As her writing made its way across the right side of the board, I noticed that her tone began to gain agency and her voice shifted slightly from passive to active. In the middle of the right side of the board, she wrote "PUSH-PULL" and boxed in this phrase as she had done with "WHY ME." On the top of the board was a quote, *Hazel, you're an irresponsible bitch.* But next to it was the statement, *I don't misuse I needa pair of shoes, now laugh all you want but this is real talk, and I laugh too but I gotta do the walk.* Under these words was the assertion, *So don't judge my shoes because they ain't new.*

This multihued stream of consciousness led to the elucidation of a narrative template that, as a class, we named the "*why me* story." On the board, Hazel had located *why me* at the center of her thinking. Her giant brainstorm pushed us to realize that we often ask *why me* when we feel overwhelmed by things too big for us, compounded by a lack of control to change them. This is especially true for young people who do not have control over many factors that influence their quality of life. It occurred to us that *why me* is sometimes the only story we know how to access. It is a fallback template that can shape how we think when we don't understand why hard life events happen. *Why me* frames these life events as happening *to* us, and it leads to a story that spins in passive voice.

Hazel's *why me* story stayed on my board for a week before I had to erase it to make space for the teacher whose classroom I shared. In the meantime, Hazel shared her thinking about *why me* with every student in our 11th grade, which led us to realize that we all have a *why me* story. Sometimes we state it outright. Sometimes it operates as a shell of anger or a veneer of indifference. Sometimes *why me* takes a life of its own and pulls us out of alignment. A problem with *why me* is the shame that tends to accompany it, so we tried to get rid of the shame.

This is how the third narrative in our curriculum evolved. First, we tried to write out part of our *why me* stories. Since we all have them, we decided that it made sense to share them. Then we tried to write them in a revised template, with the aim of writing the same experiences in a template other than *why me*, like *why not me*, or, in Hazel's case, *why them*. We called this *why me* revision.

## REVISING "WHY ME": DEFINING THE "MILKMAN MOMENT"

Hazel referred to different stages in her life in her final narrative. In this and other assignments, she addressed the "Hazel" before I knew her, before she became publicly known for writing and sharing her poetry. By the time she discovered her *why me* story, she identified solidly as a writer in and out of the classroom. Her growth lay in her reflection, and in her ability to write from a wiser perspective on her past.

In a conversation with me, Hazel pointed to herself as someone who acted out *why me* for a long time. She admitted, "*Why me* played out in the way that I stole everything. So the reason I didn't want to ask for help, you know, and that was a big part of the *why me*, because I've been stealing since I was 8, so I never wanted to ask because it's just so pitiful, and it's just so sorrowful, and so *oh poor thing, she can't do it on her own.*" In her *why me* revision, she described her earlier years when she coped with trauma through self-harm:

> I never followed the rules and allowed myself to be disciplined because I had my own way of disciplining myself which involved attempted overdoses, and constantly cutting my wrist, arms, thighs, ankles, shoulders, fingertips, and feet. I didn't want to have to even think of my initial *why me* so I made up my own that I'd have an answer to, my own that I could turn into an ineffective *why not me?* I been always too scared to face the true reasoning why and the following whys that would answer it, so I made my own that I would know how to control.

Cutting is a psychological form of running. Perry and Szalavitz (2006) identify it as a post-trauma response that induces a dissociative state. Where hyper-vigilance triggers a defensive reaction that seems overblown or out of place, dissociation is an emotional disconnection from reality that triggers numbness to emotional or physical pain. The act of cutting can create a dissociative state similar to an adaptive response that one has to an original trauma. Perry and Szalavitz explain, "Cutting can be soothing because it provides an escape from anxiety, caused by revisiting traumatic memories or just the challenges of everyday life" (p. 182).

Hazel's writing was expressive from the time that I met her, but it became more affirmative through her work in our class. As she looked back on prior points in her life, she began to explore different ways of making causal connections between her experiences and their source. Instead of pinpointing herself as the cause of her trauma, she began to see herself more as its solution. She started to recognize that her trauma self-perpetuated in part because she needed to make story revisions, and not because she was pathological. This realization helped her develop agency through writing that went beyond describing events that had happened to her and allowed her to employ evidence from her story to make an argument for a shift in her way of thinking.

As Hazel opted to confront her *why me* story directly through her final three papers, her revisions ran concurrently along academic and personal lines. Her first academic essay focused on family relationships in *Song of Solomon* between Macon II and Ruth Dead and their children, Lena, Corinthians, and Milkman. Hazel observed how both parents pass dysfunctional cycles to their children, and her title—"They May Be Scarred Forever"—was indicative of her argument. She tied the negative impact the parents have on their children to negative cycles the children inherit and argued that this impact leaves immutable scars. As she moved to her next narrative, however, she identified a *why me* template in this academic argument that rendered it problematic.

In her *why me* revision, she legitimized the *why me* story as a fundamental part of being human, and noted that "it's only our nature as humans to wonder why." She traced *why me* to her actions that deflected attention from the real issues and provided armor against vulnerability:

> My current fear of others is their fear of knowing *why me*. I know the feeling of being afraid and not wanting to know. I know the feeling of covering up the fact that you're scared with a more dominant, controlling, rebellious, careless way of life that you want to portray to others. When really inside you ARE screaming with burning unanswered questions that are weighing you down.

Hazel's revision began when she looked beyond *why me* to explore the connection between her story and the *why me* stories of her family. She reframed *why me* to a broader context—*why them*—which led her to realize that her parents both had a *why me*, which shaped how they were able to give and receive love.

> As we look deeper into *why me*, we find a new profound way of thinking. You can't escape *why me* without figuring out *why them*. It's sort of like a family tree . . . I was caught in wondering *why me* and not wanting to find out that I never took a second to realize that my mother and father both have a *why me*. I question why they treat me like that or why they do that. I should be questioning who made them think it was this way or what happened to them that transfigured them into the person they are now.

Hazel's revision helped her understand that her parents' actions were not directly about *her*, despite how personal they felt. This points to a paradoxical purpose of personal narrative. The goal is not necessarily to personalize problems, but to *depersonalize* them. Viewed through a trauma lens, Hazel's revisions help her shift her narrative from a stance of *what is wrong with me?* to one that simply asks, *what has happened?*

This shift is aligned with the work of the characters in *Song of Solomon*. Toni Morrison (Taylor-Guthrie, 1994) remarks that "racism hurts in a very personal way. Because of it, people do all sorts of things in their personal lives and love relationships" (p. 135). Hazel's ability to depersonalize her family relationships by relocating them in a broader narrative represents a merging of the personal and collective. Shor notes, "Students unaware of the connections between their own lives and society personalize their problems" (1987, p. 89). In Hazel's final academic essay, she realized that this personalization is what traps Milkman, the main character in *Song of Solomon*, in circuitous thinking about what he doesn't deserve until he understands how to change the story.

Hazel's final academic essay was a revision of her first, in that her shift from *why me* to *why them* guided her rereading of the literary text. She pushed beyond an analysis of family dysfunction to examine how Milkman makes the same narrative revision from *why me* to *why them*, which enables him to learn his family history and understand the socio-historical context that helped to shape his parents' maladjusted ways. For the first time, he can view them with compassion and recognize his responsibility to grow. In Hazel's first essay, she viewed the dysfunction of the Dead family as something that may "scar the children forever," but her second essay offered a more empowered view. She argued that Milkman's shift to *why them* forces him to search for real answers to deeper questions, as she contended, "Once we find the answers we too will fly."

These revisions were evident in key phrases that were themes in her papers, as shown in Figure 4.3.

Hazel realized through her writing that there is no answer to *why me*. Rather, its purpose may be to unlock our need to ask *why* in a way to broaden our vision. At the end of her narrative revision, she explained, "Once we find the key to the initial *why*, a whole line of responding *whys* open up into consideration. It possibly even shifts you wondering, why *not* me? Our stories are all different, some similar, some may not even be close, but we all have *why* in it. . . . I understand now that the moment when I question *why* is a moment we all have in our lifetime, and the story of *why* is in all of us."

In reference to the novel, my students and I came to name and define the "Milkman moment" as one of lucidity, as a narrative shift from *why me* to a broader frame that generates new understandings and possibilities, and as a linguistic move from the language of what we do or don't deserve to a more deeply contextualized, depersonalized articulation of our personal and social worlds.

\*   \*   \*   \*

Pennebaker and Seagal (1999) emphasize in their research that "merely having a story may not be sufficient to ensure good health. A story that may have been constructed when the person was young or in the midst of a trauma may be insufficient later in life when new information is discovered or broader perspectives are adopted. In our studies . . . the act of constructing the stories is

**Figure 4.3. Hazel's Body of Work**

| Paper | Phrase |
| --- | --- |
| What Is Love? | "I Love Love" |
| Love Narrative Template | "I'm the Reason They're Gone" |
| *SOS* Character Analysis | "They May Be Scarred Forever" |
| *Why Me* Revision | "The Story of Why Is in All of Us" |
| *SOS* Analysis and Revision | "We Too Will Fly" |

associated with mental and physical health improvement. A constructed story, then, is a type of knowledge that helps to organize the emotional effects of an experience as well as the experience itself" (p. 1249).

Hazel self-identified as a writer, and she understood better than most students how writing could lead to personal change. When I asked her to explain the connection between writing and revision, she said, "Writing is expression. And I've had a lot of moments where I'm trying to write, and I do not have words for it, and it's really frustrating, but when you do have those words . . . especially when you go back you can see where you were at one point. And you see where you've changed since writing. If you continue to write, you just see the changing in it."

In a conversation with me, she described how her writing and revisions affected how she viewed her father. She realized that it was important to consider the good with the bad, rather than rehearse the same criticisms. She explained:

> A poem this year that I decided to write, I don't know if I showed it to you, it was about my dad, and I performed it a few Saturdays ago at a poetry competition and he wasn't even there. And I got tired. Like I just looked back at all my poems, and it just turned from love to just talking so bad on my parents, which is normal. Me personally, I felt dirty. I felt that there are things that are good in both of my parents and even though the addiction overcomes that, I wanna be able to notice that also. So I finally wrote my first poem about my dad and his strength and everything, so I feel like these papers helped me realize the *why me*, and they helped me realize that my dad is the way he is for a reason, and his addiction is that way for a reason. 'Cause my dad's always told me about his childhood story and when he started. So I think my view changed a lot in my writing.

Hazel continued to reconstruct her stories through her poetry. She performed a poem with two of her classmates at the spring Showcase performance, pictured in Figure 4.4, that they decided to name *Why Me*. In a conversation at the end of the school year, she asked if she could read part of it to me. I agreed to be an audience, and then she began to read:

> I'm not alone any more.
> The bag I've been carrying for years has transfigured in my thoughts into a vast amount of epiphanies.
> What was my defeat once before turned into my victories of today.
> I was pushed so far down,
> it gave me something to build up to.
> Deprived of proper relationships like a lifeless soul,
> friction engraved into each of my spirit's wrinkles.
> I ask, why me?

**Figure 4.4. (From Left to Right) Serenity, Patrick, and Hazel at Spring Showcase Celebration**

Though I have all these relationships, my narrative soul is still single.
Searching like Scooby Doo, where are you?
I can't see without my glasses.
Can somebody help me see?
Why did I deserve this, why is this happening to me?
Why was the choice for me to struggle this much?
Finally reality hit
and we notice
that there's a why me in everyone,
so why NOT me?

## CHAPTER 5

# Revising Narrative Truth

**Truth:** *noun.* Where I get my pride and grace.
**Agency:** *noun.* The belief that I am here for a purpose. I'm not
a nobody, I'm a someone.

—Abraham's Definitions, 11th Grade English

This chapter considers how revisions to narrative truth can help a student derive constructive meaning from stories with themes of humiliation or shame. It centers on the narrative work of Abraham, who was one of my toughest students and the one I worried most about. Even now, I am not completely sure how to "write" him. The theme of truth pervaded his narratives and his personal story. His writing conveyed harsh truths that he perceived in his life that colored his sense of self, and he wrote himself as a character imprisoned by them. Over the course of his narrative work, his tone and self-characterization evolved as he realized that he had agency in deciding what truth meant to him.

The purpose of personal narrative is not to arrive at *objective* truth—since there is no such thing—but to create *narrative* truth, or what is true to us (Spence, 1982). Narrative truths are the truths we perceive, and they define our stories in ways that are central to our sense of self. Singer argues, "What ultimately matters is not the sheer number of bad events . . . to which individuals have been exposed" (2001, p. 274). What matters instead is the extent to which a writer has "configured the events of their lives into a narrative that supplied meaning and hope" (p. 274). Our well-being depends on our ability to draw wisdom and constructive meaning from even the most painful or cruel experiences, and, in our class, Abraham's narratives best represented the struggle to pull constructive meaning from a destructive story. He did this by revising his understanding of the concept of "truth."

For Abraham, school gravity was dependent on his relationship with teachers. He was adamant that he needed relationships with teachers in order to learn from them, and he would not work for teachers he did not like. When I asked him if he could learn from a teacher who he did not really know, he answered, "Well personally I can't . . . I won't. I won't let myself. I will like shut myself down and close the door." Abraham's academic success was inextricable from his ability to develop and sustain positive relationships with adults. More than any student in my class, however, he struggled to trust adults and peers, which made it tough for him to build the relationships that he needed to engage. He explained, "It's like I don't really open up to my friends or like anybody really. Only to certain people." He also had a negative association with school. He had a learning disability that had made academics a challenge for him, and he could point to few school experiences where he had felt successful, as he told me, "I felt like dropping out freshman year." Overall, he found school an alienating place.

Abraham and I built a tenuous relationship in our first few months of working together, which was a credit to both of us. We shared real conversations about real issues, and we valued each other, which could also be a trigger for either of us when conflict escalated. Our relationship could become antagonistic, but not in the traditional sense where teachers and students are disconnected or unable to relate to each other's positions. Abraham struggled to maintain closeness without eruptions of anger or distrust, and I struggled to handle conflict without taking negative emotions personally and stepping away. This dynamic between us became a pattern in the two years that this chapter captures. Our conflict was an interaction of our personal issues that we were each trying to work through and understand, and our student-teacher relationship was evidence of our common skill in reading each other's defenses and paying acute attention to signals we gave that our doors were open or closed.

## PRELIMINARY CONVERSATIONS: "IT'S WHATEVER, YOU KNOW"

Abraham stared hard at me for the first several weeks of school. He has sharp features and an intense expression, so I *felt* this look and deciphered it as his attempt to either scrutinize or unsettle me. I soon sensed that I was being studied, and I intuited that he was trying to start a conversation. He would linger after class on the fringes of the room and observe, or he would establish my doorway as a place to meet others during passing period. Eventually we started talking, and he initiated the conversation.

Abraham was one of several students who were eligible to spend a period each day in the resource room for extra academic support. There, he was supposed to work in a small group setting or one-on-one with the resource specialist, whose job was to support kids diagnosed with learning disabilities. Our school used a full-inclusion model, meaning that the resource specialist collaborated with students' core subject teachers to make academic accommodations and support their work in the general education classroom. Abraham's resource period was fifth, and he had astutely figured out that this period was my prep, so he began a pattern of finding me in my room at this hour. The routine was usually the same: he would ask the resource teacher for permission to come to my room to work on assignments, and about 10 minutes into the period she would call to ask if this was okay. Moments later a shadow would appear in my doorway, where he would wait for an invitation to come in. Sometimes I would talk with him for 10 to 20 minutes before dutifully trying to redirect him to the work he was supposed to do. Other times I would sit next to him and work through an assignment with him, especially if it was one from my class. This was a useful way to ensure that he would attempt my work, and it allowed me a valuable glimpse into his academic dexterity and his thought processes. Then there were days when we would just talk, and when this seemed like quality time that was important enough to both of us to make a priority.

These one-on-one sessions were valuable from an academic and behavioral standpoint. I grew to appreciate the sharpness of Abraham's mind, and I also learned that it could be a challenge to get him to produce anything of quality. His attention span was short, and he would grow impatient with himself or with me if he got stuck on his work. This was a particular issue with writing. Asking him to elaborate or rewrite something could trigger a reaction where he took criticism personally and dismissed an assignment completely. Working effectively with him meant walking a line between challenging him and accidentally pushing him away, so I learned to structure his feedback based on a constant risks-benefits assessment of whether it would have the desired effect or make me lose my leverage.

The time that Abraham and I spent talking and working one-on-one also helped me learn how to engage him constructively in a group setting. If Abraham was uncooperative, the whole class would feel it, and our relationship gave me the leverage I needed to redirect him publicly without sparking an argument—at least, most of the time. Overall, I observed that Abraham's behavior tended to create a pattern of highs and lows in relationships with people he genuinely seemed to like. Some days, he actively engaged in my class and wanted to please me, which contributed to the flow of things in a way that made me feel like a better teacher. On other days, he would grow negative, explode in anger, or walk out of class. There were stretches when our relationship was rocky, and some of his outbursts felt excruciatingly mean. I had to step out of the room one day to collect myself when he glared at me mid-lesson and told me that I was pathetic. His remorse followed within the hour, and the dean and I spent the next two days convincing him to return to my class while he crucified himself for having ruined it.

Abraham's mood was unpredictable, and he bore a certain contempt that was difficult to read. In many ways, he fit the profile of a student whose actions in many schools would lead to exclusionary discipline, like suspension or referral out of class. His demeanor was resonant with Bruce Perry's description of "people [who] believe that others can 'sense' that they are 'unworthy' or 'bad' . . . they project their self-hate onto the world and become sensitized—indeed, hypersensitive—to any signs of rejection" (2006, p. 195). Abraham was also gang-affiliated and had had negative encounters with police. He worried that he would be incarcerated at a future point. He was quick to fight with anyone he perceived as disrespectful. Our administration and I knew that we needed to handle these incidents with concern for how the messaging would affect his sense of self. Students who have negative encounters with law enforcement and school can internalize the labels put on them and defensively embrace the stigma that comes with being "deviant" (Rios, 2011). It was critical that we communicated caring. We wanted to disengage Abraham from disruptive behaviors, but we did not want to disengage him as a person. We *did* want to engage him as a student, which required us to provide learning experiences that would show him how education could bring self-awareness and other tools to ease the pain.

These tools were precisely what I hoped the narrative curriculum in our class would offer him. The tool that seemed most helpful by its end was the notion of "truth," which emerged the first time in a conversation we had about one of his papers, when I asked him if there anything he felt he had left out or wanted to explain more. His answer was that he wanted to learn how to "how to put the good and the bad together," by focusing more on "more good times than bad" without "covering up the bad times." This led us to a conversation that I detail later in the chapter about finding truth in the balance between the positive and negative aspects of our lives.

Abraham engaged with all of the writing assignments, and he grew more and more engrossed in the novel as we came to its end. The writing that he did in the first few weeks lent evidence to suggest that something in his self-narrative led to his self-contempt, which in turn influenced his relationship patterns. Early in the curriculum, he began to express his internal angst through cryptic words. On an open-response in which I asked students about their early impressions of *Song of Solomon*, he wrote:

> In *Song of Solomon*, most of the characters have deep secrets that can
> end lives and I can relate to that. I have secrets that just won't come
> out. And the reason I at times don't like to listen or do homework
> is because it doesn't just bring back bad memories, it feels like I'm
> replaying the moment. If this helps at all. I grew up with my sister,
> my brother, mom and dad. As the years passed by secrets have been
> revealed that kinda hurt me in different ways. But I just never showed
> it and if I tell my mom what's bothering me she will be like *get over it*.
> I don't feel like saying what it is because it's whatever, you know. Over
> the years it just became locked away.

The first time I read these lines, I naturally wondered what *it* was, and while it was not my business to know, I wondered to what extent *it* underlay his manner and the stress in our relationship. This writing was not the first time that Abraham alluded to something he kept to himself. He spent the first 17 months in our conversations referring to his "secrets" without elucidating what they were, and I never directly asked him.

## THE ANTI-STORY: "LORD PLEASE ERASE MY BIRTHDATE"

The people who come to see us bring us their stories. They hope they tell them well enough so that we understand the truth of their lives. They hope we know how to interpret their stories correctly.

—Robert Coles, *The Call of Stories*

Abraham's initial love narrative stated squarely, "I hate the truth."

While he did not pinpoint what the "truth" was, his references to it seemed to identify it as a source of shame. He wrote, "I hate the truth. I close my heart, my past is deep, I can't look at a mirror, I can't even sleep." Truth functioned metaphorically in his writing as a force that seemed to imprison him in his own story. He craved it even as it haunted him. I would later learn that there were two main parts to this "truth." He would reveal one part in his narrative template and the other in his *why me* revision. The first hard truth would deal with learning who his mother was, and the second hard truth would deal with learning about his father. He doubted whether it was better to know the truth when the truth was hard to know, and his sequence of papers questioned how someone could confront hard truths without self-destructing.

Abraham's first love narrative was fragmented and obscure, and it revealed only shards of information. His words had a tone of self-sabotage and he referenced a character named "MA," but there was no plot. Nor was there sufficient context in his lines, "Hey 'MA' are we family or just friends, cause this thought and feeling never ends. I wish this feeling fades away, it's building like a box of hate. Everytime I wanna tell you I love you, I hesitate. Sometimes I wish I was never made Lord please erase my birthdate." Abraham spoke of a love that seemed beyond his grasp to actualize, and he rejected a truth that seemed to have power over him, rather than the other way around. This truth seemed to render his existence somehow wrong. The only agency that his narrative offered him was the ability to rid the world of his existence. He also appealed to a source outside of himself to do this in the line, "Lord please erase my birthdate."

Abraham's first love narrative revealed an association with "truth" that undermined his ability to see himself as deserving of love or compassion. His writing veered toward what Singer (2001) calls the "anti-story," or a default pattern of thinking that takes agency in saying "fuck it"—as a substitute for resilience—when we lack a better story. This anti-story subsumed his sense of self in the lines that read, "If I had the chance to change my identity I would just to make my family happy. . . . I notice when I get mad I erupt without a reason. I get madder my feeling's deep in." Gregory Boyle writes in *Tattoos on the Heart*, "Resilience is born by grounding yourself in your own loveliness" (2010, p. 94). Abraham struggled with resilience because his story grounded him in anger and self-aversion. His own loveliness was not something that he believed in. To build resilience, he would need to revise his meaning of truth to one that grounded him more deeply in love.

While Abraham's narrative was hard to understand, its theme of rejection was clear. It conveyed a fractured self-relationship that hid between the lines. It was fragile because its destructive and disintegrative elements threatened to overwhelm it. It needed hope to fortify a different reading of truth.

*     *     *     *

Maxine Greene contends that personal narrative writing can "provide occasions . . . for a reaching out towards alternative ways of being human, of being in the world" (1994, p. 24). It can offer students the chance to "articulate the themes of their existence" until they can "name what has been up to then obscure" (1978, p. 18–19). Her words capture Abraham's slow struggle to revise his concept of truth from a life sentence to a more malleable interpretation of events.

Abraham's second love narrative—his template—opened with the words, "When I look back at this I see and feel reality, then it turns to horror. My whole life's been feeling like this for quite a while." After his opening reference to "this," however, he shifted from the vague language of his prior narrative to more substantive content. The language that shielded the truth began to dissolve, and a more complete story emerged as he began to break it down: "See I grew up with my grandma raising me. When I was small I always thought that she was my biological mom . . . till she broke it down to me at the age of ten." He downplayed this statement with the words, "It was whatever," and continued with the narrative:

> Because half of my childhood my grandma always told me that my real mom was my sister. As I started growing up I started asking questions like *who really gave birth to me? Who's my read dad?* I would never receive an answer. I would ask my other family members but they would shut down on me.

Abraham created a storyboard with drawings and captions to illustrate his narrative template. His first storyboard scene portrayed his mother handing him to his grandmother to raise. He was a wrapped-up, faceless bundle who was passed between two unsmiling women.

1. Real mom had me. She had to give me up to her mom. My mom
   was 17.

The second storyboard read, "Grandma raised me, real mom forgotten."
The drawing showed a small child saying, "Love you mom," and an adult
figure who replied, "Yo tambien."

2. Grandma raised me. Real mom forgotten.

The third scene simply read, "THE TRUTH." The image depicted an adult
telling an older child, "I'm not your real mom," and the child's response read
simply as a question mark. The figures in this drawing were different from the
previous two in that the faces had no features. They were blank.

3. The TRUTH.

The fourth scene read, "Hell breaks loose." There were no people in this drawing. Inside a box, Abraham drew a diagonal squiggly line that he slashed through with a thicker, straight line.

4. Hell breaks loose.

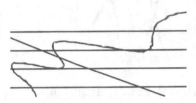

In the process of trying to uncover information about his family, Abraham discovered a disturbing truth. The woman who he thought was his mother was not—she was his grandmother, and his mother was someone who he previously knew as his sister. His interpretation of "hell breaks loose" aligned with an image of crossed-out empty space. Abraham's love narrative template depicted a turning point, and he did not know how to pull constructive meaning from it.

A turning point is defined as a pivotal moment that signifies a change in our life course (Schultz, 2001). How we choose to narrate a turning point is important. It can instill resilience or stymie our progress and growth (McAdams & Bowman, 2001). Once again, the defining principle is that our experience matters less to our well-being than how we interpret it, and I wanted to emphasize this to Abraham, so I asked him to talk about his paper with me one-on-one. The conversation went as follows:

*Ms. LaMay:* What would you wanna add to that paper, if there's anything you feel like you left out, or didn't get to, or wanted to explain more about?

*Abraham:* Um, the good times me and my mom had. Like, ok, when you read this paper did it seem negative or positive?

*Ms. LaMay:* It seemed like you were looking at things and trying to frame them. So you're saying you would actually write in there some of the good times too?

*Abraham:* More good times than bad. But then that's covering up the bad times.

*Ms. LaMay:* It could be but it doesn't have to be because it's interesting how we choose to write our stories. Know what I mean? I could write my story like it was one big tragedy. I could write my story like things were fine. And in a sense both stories are, have truth to them. But how do I capture what was most true to me—by balancing those stories out? 'Cause you know that paper that I gave you guys that was part of my memoir with my baby pictures in it and stuff?

*Abraham:* Um hm.

*Ms. LaMay:* Like there were parts where I just, I wanted to write my mom, I wanted to capture some of her charm, I wanted to capture some of her quirkiness that was kind of actually funny, um, and I didn't just want to focus on how messed up she was. But I think I definitely struggled with how to balance those two. Like the bad can overcome the good in your life but then how you choose to use those memories to frame them as being, you know *my life is fucked up* versus *from this experience I'm drawing a meaning that allows me to think positively about my ability to overcome things.* See what I'm saying? Totally different conclusions drawn from the story.

In my conversations with Abraham about his writing, I did not assume a therapist role, nor did he ask me to. Newkirk (1997) identifies a paradox about personal narratives—that their therapeutic value may lie in our refusal to treat them as "*directly* therapeutic" (p. 20). I did not ask Abraham to think about *what* he was writing as much as *how* he was writing and which strategies he was using to interpret and convey meaning. My approach paralleled a curricular method like Schoenbach, Greenleaf, and Murphy's (2012) *Reading for Understanding*, or Kylene Beers' (2003) *When Kids Can't Read*, where the focus is not to probe students' memory of a text, but to engage them in a discussion of how they are reading, and focus them on metacognitive strategies they use to make meaning. Along these lines, I wanted to raise Abraham's awareness of the strategies he was semi-consciously using as a writer and to help him develop and own these so he could find more control in how he constructed his story.

Rather than ask Abraham directly about his story's content, I tried to direct his attention to the perspectives that he took, so he knew where he could focus to revise. Patricia Stock argues that the process of writing can serve a therapeutic role for a student, and she defines her role as "[confirming] that her work demonstrated she was learning to entertain from multiple perspectives concerns she had once seen from only one perspective" (1995, p. 77). I suspected that if Abraham could find points of agency through his perspective, then he could gain a stronger sense of control over his story, instead of wrestling with a story that seemed to be controlling him.

Abraham's academic writing played an important role in this process. He carried his narrative themes of truth and love into the essays he wrote on the character Guitar, whose alienation and anger he could relate to. His interest in this character's thinking was the reason why he became more invested in the novel toward the end. He was particularly intrigued by Guitar's painful sense of betrayal by someone he had considered his close friend and brother. Abraham understood why this led Guitar to show his love through "what he believes in and what he fights for and . . . just his mentality in life. And how he tries to help out others but in really hard core ways." When I asked Abraham later if his essays on Guitar had affected his thinking about himself or his life, he replied, "I'm here for a purpose, I guess. I need to do something and I'm not a nobody, I'm a someone. That's it."

Abraham's academic work was key to his narrative's revision, and in his essays, he conveyed awareness that painful experience can profoundly impact how we give and receive love. In his analysis of Guitar, he wrote, "Love in some cases is too strong for a person to recognize and accept." He argued for an interpretation of Guitar as a well-intentioned character whose struggle to deal with hard truths is misunderstood and whose love is misguided but true. He identified Guitar as an example of how anger can twist love into forms that are hard to recognize. He explained, "This can happen to people in a way that gets them confused about what they're doing and how they try to do it." He argued that Guitar's need to prove his legitimacy in the conditions he had been dealt could drive him—or anyone—to extreme actions, which could explain why Guitar "crosses the line and doesn't recognize it." The concluding lines of his analysis read, "Guitar has helped me in real life deal with searching for the truth and accepting it in my personal life. I will stand my ground and not let this pain overcome my goals."

## RESILIENT TRUTHS: "WHERE I GET MY PRIDE AND GRACE"

When young people begin to feel that their lives are insubstantial, it's hard to convince them that this is only a phase in a stage of their lives, that they are meant to overcome all this, to overcome the idealizations and delusions and come to grips with their own makeup and that of the world.

—Luis Rodriguez, *Hearts and Hands: Creating Community in Violent Times*

Our class practice of sharing writing had a noticeable impact on Abraham. The school gravity this practice held for him arose from the extent to which he genuinely craved feeling part of a family and community. He had trouble building the sense of family that he wanted in his life because it was not within his power to do so. He had trouble building the sense of community that he needed because his trust issues interfered with his personal relationships. David Johnson and Roger Johnson (2004) maintain that one of the two most important social and emotional competencies is *interpersonal effectiveness*, or the degree to which the outcomes of our interactions with others match our intentions. The authors stress that someone's interpersonal effectiveness "largely determines the quality and course of his or her life" (p. 41). Abraham wanted to cultivate meaningful relationships with others that he did not always feel empowered to build. Our practice of sharing writing helped him use writing as a kind of substitute for in-person interactions that could become confrontations. Writing was a way of communicating in our class that offered him acceptance and an invitation to join the community. So he began to offer to share his writing, and he essentially wrote his way into our class dialogue in a way that profoundly changed the experience for all of us.

On another note, Abraham and I went through one of the most tumultuous periods in our relationship a few weeks after our conversation about the positive and negative balance of truth. Our conflict and its escalation in class would usually follow a storyline that went something like this: Abraham would say something to me or emit an attitude that I interpreted as dismissive of me or my teaching. I would take this personally and push back by being a victim and putting emotional distance between us to communicate that my feelings were hurt. He would take this personally and get angry. He would then begin to challenge me directly or make comments under his breath. I would take this personally and not know what to do, at which point my flight response would kick in and I would try to resist the urge to send him out of class. Catching myself here was important. I was the adult in the situation, but I would quickly get triggered in these moments, and my default pattern of communication (withdrawal) would kick in, which usually worked well to escalate his default pattern of communication (anger), and so it would go. He was the student who, without trying to, called me out consistently on my own detrimental tendencies by churning them up and then handing me a figurative mirror to look at myself.

Our learned behaviors around conflict tied to both of our love narratives and templates. Fortunately, the curriculum offered us the opportunity to talk about our battles on this deeper level. I was not the only teacher who had conflict with Abraham, but the intensity of our desire to hurt and feel hurt by each other came from the fact that it was a relationship we both cared about, which was, on the "love template" level, a trigger for us both. It seemed to me that Abraham sometimes had an impulse to antagonize teachers to their breaking point and then take their rejection of him personally. It was crucial for me to remember in these moments that he was *handing me an invitation* to validate the stories of rejection that he held about himself. The fact that I was someone whose judgment he cared about meant that I got these invitations more frequently. I could treat them as rule violations and send him out of class, or I could choose to see them as solicitations that came from a place of pain and unconsciously attempted to prove the legitimacy of his line, "Sometimes I wish I was never made Lord please erase my birthdate."

In the psychological literature, this pattern of behavior ties to a construct called the "internal working model," originally developed by John

Bowlby (1973). Our internal working model links our self-image with the people we want to attach it to, in a way that assumes and often produces a familiar story. Internal working models originate from the interpersonal dynamics that mark our early developmental years. Researchers suggest that "a child who experiences—and hence represents—attachment figures as primarily rejecting, is likely to form a complementary working model of the self as unworthy or acceptable" (Greenberg, Cichetti, & Cummings, 1990, p. 275). To be effective in the moments of conflict that surfaced with Abraham, I needed to respond to his anger with a disconfirming stance that did not reject *him,* but did reject the *story* that was operating in him in that moment. This meant that I had to remain conscious enough of my actions to refuse to respond with the rejection that his actions were seeking. The problem was that my *own* internal working model also had an impulse to seek out and read rejection onto conflict situations, which compelled me to take his actions personally in a way that made it difficult for me to "show up" calmly. Abraham and I were both stubborn, and we were masters at targeting each other's weak spots. This explains why, on a fundamental level, we were also able to challenge each other on uncomfortable intrapersonal work.

Abraham's case is important because he represents a student who tries and often succeeds in receiving disciplinary measures that can result in suspension or expulsion. The problem is that school discipline is traditionally structured in a way that plays directly into the interpersonal dynamics that I just described. Pedro Noguera, who has written extensively on this topic, argues that "the marginalization of students who are frequently punished occurs because schools rely primarily on two strategies to discipline students who misbehave: humiliation and exclusion" (2008, p. 133). Humiliation and rejection *were the exact themes* that lay at the core of Abraham's love narratives. Punitive discipline policies are usually ineffective with students like Abraham because they reinforce over and over again the self-story that is driving the behavior. They aim to teach a simplistic form of cause and effect, in that students should come to see how their misbehavior causes consequences in the "real world." Yet most students already know this, and the shallowness of the approach is dangerous for a student with Abraham's mindset, because it circumvents the root cause of his behavior—embedded in the line "if I had the chance to change my identity I would"—and inadvertently reinforces the causal connection implicit in his story that *who he is* causes problems. Abraham's love narratives and consequent behavior patterns illustrate a principal point: disciplinary measures that employ humiliation and exclusion to address behaviors that stem from internalized humiliation and exclusion are not only counterproductive, they are unethical. Yet they are what many schools do. They embody our larger systemic inclination toward consequences and punishment that compels the increased marginalization and potential incarceration of young people like Abraham.

At Escenario, I was fortunate to work with administrators who intuitively understood these social justice issues. As a teacher, I was given administrative and counseling support to push conversations with students about root causes of their actions in a way that could translate to real learning experiences for them—and for me. A shortcoming of traditional discipline is that it does not connect consequences to learning in a way that teaches a moral lesson or ties to the educational mission of schools (Noguera, 2003, 2008). Noguera contends, "[Exclusionary] strategies . . . do little to enable students to learn from their mistakes and develop a sense of responsibility for their behavior" (2008, p. 133). Every student in this book exemplifies how we can better influence changes in behavior if we help students build and sustain school gravity in their relationships with school and education. Moreover, Abraham's sense of responsibility for his actions was inextricable from his sense of agency that he mattered in the world, and that his desire to be accountable would make a difference.

The concepts and strategies embedded in the narrative curriculum were my approach to classroom discipline for Abraham. I believed that he could more easily learn from his behavior if he could connect it to the templates in his meaning of love and develop a sense of agency in his interactions with those he cared about. I wanted to deal with our conflict by engaging him in conversation about its root causes, rather than rely on positional power in a way that would hold no real power with him. Although my vision for this was clear, I still struggled in the day-to-day work to transform the tension that kept recurring between us. A few weeks after spring break, Abraham and I had a series of disagreements that intensified to the point where we had a mediation in the counselor's office. This led to my decision to take a break from our conversations outside of class. As was my pattern, I responded to his anger by putting distance in our relationship. I found out later that Abraham was almost arrested around this same time. He told me several weeks afterwards that he was caught with an illegal weapon and could have had a charge of resisting arrest. He explained, "Yeah 'cause I ran . . . and then I think the cop kind of knew me so he kind of turned it down to a misdemeanor. And I guess I now have counseling 'cause I asked for it." I asked him at this point if he would have taken the counseling option a year ago, and he said, "I would have denied it. I wouldn't even have liked to hear that word."

Meanwhile, right at the time when students began working on their *why me* revisions, Abraham and I were at a communication impasse. He was the one who reached out to me and broke it. This explains why his third personal narrative began as a text message. Two nights after our mediation, he texted to tell me that he had started the *why me* revision. He told me that he had written it as a Google doc that he had just shared with me. He wanted to know if I would read it and tell him if it was what I wanted. I read his first few paragraphs and wrote him back and told him to keep working because I was excited about it. It looked to be a more exhaustive paper than any of his that I had seen.

The next night, he texted that he had finished and he asked again if I would read it. He also told me that he wanted me to share it with everyone in class the next day. I asked if he wanted to remove his name, and he said no, because he wanted everyone to know his story, and he knew that someone in our class would learn from reading it.

So the next day, I turned his narrative into a class set of copies. When I passed it out, I did not tell the students whose it was, because I knew that they would quickly figure this out. Our usual protocol for sharing student writing was to read it out loud. Either a student would read, or I would. But for Abraham's paper, I decided to tell them to read it silently to themselves, because I wanted each student to have his or her own private experience with it.

As students read, the response in the room was palpable. In his opening, he revealed the "truth" he had alluded to many times.

> See my story begins with me laying on my mother's lap, confused as fuck and only eleven years old. Mom was just bursting into tears. I just saw fear and mercy in every tear that would drop. She would look at me with a blank stare that I will always remember along with the words that came out of her mouth. "YO NO SOY TU MAMA ABRAHAM," meaning *I'm not your mom Abraham*. At first I felt like it was just a joke, but I saw more tears. I said in Spanish then, *who's my real mom?* My mom couldn't take it. She hung in there and said the sister you think that's your sister is actually your mom. I replayed, but she's only 29. Confusing right. Imagine how I felt?! Basically the mom I thought that was my mom is grandma and her daughter is my real mom. They tell me this at age 11.

He continued:

> I started to question who's my real dad. I asked my grandma, I asked my aunt. I would get different stories every time. At one point I think I even asked my real mom and she just said *fuck him he's dead*. I hated it, I wanted the damn truth . . . There was one solution in my book. Gangs and drugs. This was where the change was beginning for the worst. I started to graffiti my feelings out while hanging out with the gangs and doing drugs for quite a while. Still today I might be on this path. All I wanted is the truth.

Then the second part of his story read as follows.

> One day I was sitting in my great grandma's home with my grandma and my ex-girlfriend. We were sitting conversating. I don't know how the theory of who and where is my real dad. At this moment it became too real. My grandma that I still call mom told me without hesitation

that *your mom was raped and you're the child of that rape.* I felt so empty, angry, rebellious and enraged at everything that was in my view. I got up and walked to the bathroom crying like a baby. I couldn't look at the mirror. I felt disgusted in my face, my body, everything.

This was the core of the internal narrative, laced with humiliation and shame.

Toward the end of his narrative, Abraham made a slight revision from rejection to affirmation. He wrote, "She could have aborted me but didn't. And that's where I get my pride and grace." This was his first revision of truth. There were hard truths that he could not change, but he could adjust his construal of what they mean. He had accepted that truth was what he chose to interpret, and his agency lay in his power to define. The second-to-last sentence read, "This is what made me just open new space in my brain to understand everything." This was the "Milkman moment," when Abraham pulled his own truths to open his mind to stories he had never considered as possible accounts of experience.

As Boyle notes, "Love . . . doesn't melt who you are, but who you are not" (2010, p. 103).

**Figure 5.1. "He ran back to Solomon's store and caught a glimpse of himself in the plate glass window. He was grinning. His eyes were shining. He was as eager and happy as he had ever been in his life."**

When Abraham shared this essay, the other students embraced him and we captured the moment on film. I turned the photo in Figure 5.1 into a slide, and I wrote beneath it the line from *Song of Solomon* that captures Milkman's revelation at the end of Chapter 12: "He ran back to Solomon's store and caught a glimpse of himself in the plate-glass window. He was grinning. His eyes were shining. He was as eager and happy as he had ever been in his life."

## RESTORING LOVE: CHANGING OUR WAYS OF CARING

And so the voices at the margins get heard and the circle of compassion widens. Souls feeling their worth, refusing to forget that we belong to each other.

—Gregory Boyle, *Tattoos on the Heart*

A goal of restorative justice is to pull students in to school and education, rather than push them out the door and farther away from seeing school as a resource to work through life problems. George Galvis, the founder of Communities United for Restorative Youth Justice, maintains that restorative justice is not "an initiative or a neat new program or curriculum. It's a way of life and a way of being with each other. It's really about how we rebalance" (Yale, 2015).

The philosophies of restorative justice are rooted in indigenous traditions. They are relevant to Abraham's story and the challenges he confronted to grow as a person and student. A key principle of restorative justice is that violations in the school context are not just violations of institutional rules but are instead violations of people, relationships, and communities (Zehr, 2002). The rights of both victims and perpetrators matter. Terms like these allow a student like Abraham to connect his actions in school to his ability to build the sense of family and community he craved. A restorative approach focuses on who has been harmed in an incident and what individuals and communities may need from others to repair this harm (Zehr, 2002). These emphases hit at the heart of the interpersonal dynamics at play in human relationships and should lead to authentic conversations that can keep students like Abraham believing in school and education as a positive force in their lives.

Through the narrative curriculum, I hoped that the students and I could together create a restorative class community that would provide academic support and school gravity for Abraham. This support was most evident when Abraham's classmates responded to his *why me* revision with a disconfirming stance—in other words, they responded to his story of rejection by confirming his belonging. Abraham's writing, and his desire to share it so that others could learn, allowed him to play an important role in our class. This sense of community was the most important school gravity factor for him, because his desire to develop and sustain positive relationships was such a vital part of his will to connect.

Abraham also appreciated the growth he watched other students in the class make, and he discussed this with me: "I notice in my friends who are in the class, that I seen them doing a lot of writing too . . . like, most of them like last year they wouldn't do a lot, and now that I see them with papers, busting out papers, it's like wow they improved a lot you know, I'm not the only one improving, they're the ones improving too."

Abraham's effort to use writing to revise his understanding of truth tied to changes he perceived in himself as a writer and a person. Prior to the 11th grade, Abraham did not consider himself a writer. He told me in one of our conversations, "I wouldn't even like carrying a pencil with me." Over the course of our work together, Abraham began to use writing on his own to work his way through difficult thoughts. He explained to me, "It was like a diary, like keeping it inside it was bad for me, I didn't like it, I felt kind of trapped. But letting it out and just reading over it and reading over it, it just like, made me feel better kind of like if I was talking to like myself." Writing was a tool that helped Abraham dialogue with himself, and at one point in our conversation, he patted the paper next to him and said, "It's like if I had another me right here." Abraham also spent time rereading his own writing. When I asked him how it felt to reread work that carried strong emotions, he answered, "I didn't like reading over it but then I had to face it, you know? It was my past and it's still kind of like my future."

Abraham also made a connection between his writing and his ability to process his thoughts in a way that helped his clarity of mind: "I feel like I can think more clearly through bad times or . . . I can process what I want to think about more easily. Like last year I couldn't really process anything like I wouldn't let myself or I wouldn't function right. Even if I wanted to try to write about it, I wouldn't be able to think that well. But now it's like . . . I read over it and I was like *wow I actually did this?*" Like Hazel, Abraham was able to see himself on the written page. His tendency to reread his writing gave him a sense of his changes as a person, and the more he wrote, the easier the writing process came to him: "I can see my full potential in the paper. Something I can write pages and pages without even noticing. That's how it is for me . . . it's a new identity. Old identity, new identity. And I believe that I changed a lot."

A notable change occurred in our student-teacher relationship after Abraham shared his *why me* revision with the class. Through the remainder of the school year, we both noticed that our conflicts somewhat ceased, and we had fewer troubles communicating with each other. From Abraham's perspective, he told me, "I think what you're doing is real teaching. You called me out . . . then I was just, I wasn't in a shell no more. I was out. Doors open." From my perspective, I felt that Abraham pushed me to the top of my teaching game and pushed me to notice how I reacted to conflict. As I mentioned, we were both stubborn, and this could play out in positive ways because neither of us wanted to step back from the challenges that we posed to each other. The song "Under Pressure," by Queen and David Bowie, ends with the lyric that "love dares you to change our way of caring about ourselves," and this is essentially what Abraham and I did—we dared each other to change our way of caring to a degree that was slightly intimidating. At the same time, neither of us was comfortable admitting defeat. In the end, our stubbornness worked to our advantage and helped us manage to redefine the terms of the game, so that if one of us appeared to care more, we both "won" without either of us having to concede.

On the second-to-last day of the school year, Abraham handed me a paper that expressed how some of his feelings about school had changed. It read:

Education to me felt like a deathtrap. At the start of this year my attitude was nasty and not willing to make an effort. I would do unreasonable things just to get out of class. I would push my teachers way over the edge to make my day, because that's how it normally started. It all changed from the start of this year.

I never saw myself having a relationship with school, one because it was boring, two because I felt like it wouldn't take me nowhere. Three, I been going for all my life! I felt like a robot listening to teachers that in some ways I felt didn't care about me. So as years passed I started to change for the worst. Angry was the mindset.

Now in high school with a mindset of *I don't give a fuck*. It was hopeless. It got worse. I used teachers as a stress reliever. With too many problems at home I couldn't take problems on a paper. Many teachers gave effort to help but no I didn't want to recognize it. One teacher out of the bunch stood her ground and pushed back.

This teacher is a kind teacher. One that I would hate to lose contact with. We started off on the wrong foot. I was really mean and gave her so much trouble. I felt like I was the stress factor. She would take it. Till one day she started talking back and taking control. Constantly hitting me in my weak spot. I got worse to the point where she didn't want me in her class. This made me realize she gave it her all to make a change for the better. I would sit at home crying like a baby just thinking how stupid I was. Milkman moment!

School is now a pull factor in my life.
School is now a must if you want to succeed in life.
School is my only way out of this gruesome pain.
School is the only way to stop this pain.
With school I know I'll gain to stop the rain.

## CHAPTER 6

# Colonel Sanders, Counterplot, and "The Connect"

**Counterplot:** *noun*. Things that force you to have a mentality already. Like what's in you and why you do things. And it's hard to see it in your own life because you really just see things as having to be like that.

—Serenity's Definition, 11th Grade English

**Revise:** *verb*. To get deeper meanings out of things.

—Diego's Definition, 11th Grade English

Diego's writing at the start of the curriculum revealed a lack of ambiguity and a conviction that life struggle is deterministic. His shifts in his views about love paralleled shifts in his relationship with school and his sense that he could meaningfully engage on terms that felt compatible with his vision and outlook. His narrative work helped him move from being defined by struggle, to finding connections between school and self that translated to a stance of inquiry and encouraged his desire to take school seriously. He gradually began to rebuild the relationship with education that was a prerequisite for him to consider it relevant to his personal goals. As he began to feel a sense of agency through education, he increasingly found ways to engage with different disciplines on his own terms and to form his own educational philosophies.

I was collecting papers one afternoon when I picked up Diego's classwork and noticed a large doodle that seemed to say something important. It started at the bottom of his page and ran up the side until it crossed the top of the page upside down. It read:

We are trained with the mentality of making something out of nothing. If we have struggled so much in our life, why do we jump on it when people offer us more struggle? Are we really just trained to go with the things that we know so well?

Diego's attempts to reconcile his conflicting feelings about struggle were at the core of his relationships with the topic of love and with school. Initially, he did not perceive struggle as academic in nature. It was a battle fought in the "real world" from which school was disconnected. His personal and academic writing helped him to broaden his definition of struggle to the point where he included educators who were fighting to teach in a relevant way in a system that was not structured to reach all students. He began to realize that meaningful struggle could take many forms that were, to him, equally legitimate.

Diego's narrative revisions and his excavation of what we called *counterplot* helped him to develop a stronger sense that directing his energy toward school could complement his desire to engage in learning and thinking on a deep level. A counterplot is an internalized narrative template that can act like an undertow on our life trajectory. The term is from literary criticism. Geoffrey Hartman (1958) drew on it to explain the interrelationship of narratives in John Milton's *Paradise Lost*. My student Serenity defined a counterplot as "the things that force you to have a mentality already. Like what's in you and why you do things. And it's hard to see it in your own life because you really just see things as having to be like that." Diego defined a counterplot similarly as a story that gets *in* us when we don't know how it got there. He explained, "It's hard to see the story underneath your own. Most would like to say there isn't one, that there's no deeper reason why they do what they do, other than the obvious. It took me a while to realize why I found myself in the same situation so many times . . . There are so many stories buried underneath stories. Like a puppet master they manipulate us. It's often the things we do to prevent something from happening that let it happen."

Our class focus on counterplot led to an essential question that pervaded Diego's writing and our class dialogue: *Do we shape our stories, or do our stories shape us?*

## "SKY'S PLAN" AND THE CHARTER SCHOOL WORLD

When I first met Diego, he was set in his mind that he was going to follow in his brother's footsteps and become a Marine. He later told me that if someone had handed him the papers to sign his freshman year, he would have signed them right then and there. He did not see education playing a pivotal role in his future. As a result, he fumbled through most of his assignments without expecting to learn and spent his schooldays half asleep.

He did not attempt the first several papers that I assigned to his 10th-grade class. His first essay came toward the end of fall semester, and it was called "Sky's Plan." In it, he wrote:

Since his fam is in the military Sky feels he should join the military, even though him and his brother have arguments about it. He has made up his mind about it and in a way is already preparing. . . . Sky has a goal and as long as he reaches it, all the people that say he can't or shouldn't don't matter. Sky plans on graduating high school, not with a 4.0 for what he has in mind, it's not required you see. He designed this plan for someone lazy like himself, so a 2.0 will do. After the slow process of graduating Sky will go to college but not to expand his job possibilities like most. No he already knows what he wants and he will get it. He plans on taking advantage of the ROTC program which is available at most colleges . . . After a two year experience he will go to officer boot camp which is what any military recruiter would love for anyone to do.

Diego had a reputation among our staff as a master jokester. He was one of the quickest, most intelligent students that many of us knew, but he tended to channel his wit into his wisecracks. I observed fairly quickly that Diego had a knack for turning my assignments on their head. Over our first 6 months together, I collected work samples that I found alternately amusing and frustrating. For one of these, I asked my students to work in groups to create a "vocabulary advertisement." The point was for them to use all of their vocabulary words in written or visual context. Diego's group initially fooled around, until after several visits to their table, I finally got them working. About 10 minutes later, I began to hear eruptions of laughter from their corner, and Diego signaled me over and handed me a paper on which he had used all of the words in writing. As the best artist in our class, he had also added a drawing. The advertisement was for Viagra. Its opening lines read, "Do you reminisce for the days when you were young and audacious? Viagra will give you something colossal to be narcissistic about," and so on. I did notice that he had incorporated all of the words correctly in his parody of my assignment. I aimed for a balance between pushing him and tripping the switch that would make him never do my assignments again, and I asked his group to create another one that would be appropriate to put on the wall. However, I never received the "appropriate" version.

Each semester at our school, we were required to give students a benchmark exam in each subject. In the fall of their sophomore year, my students took the network-wide writing benchmark for English. I was annoyed when I read the writing prompt because I already sensed that it invited a shallow regurgitation of historical clichés: *Describe an historical figure who you admire and explain the important contributions that this person has made.* As could be predicted, several students wrote about Cesar Chavez and Martin Luther King, Jr. Diego, daring to be different, chose to write about Colonel Sanders, the founder of Kentucky Fried Chicken. He argued that the Colonel was underappreciated as a leader in the fast food industry, and he invented "facts" about the Colonel's life story to defend his claim. His paper had an introduction and one-and-a-half body paragraphs, which fizzled into a punctuation-less void as he ran out of interest and things to say.

One of my biggest debates with Diego was about reading. I brought him books that were tried and true with some other students, like Claude Brown's *Manchild in the Promised Land* and Jimmy Santiago Baca's *A Place to Stand*, but when we read silently, I was unable to get him to do anything but sit and stare at the wall. I tried repeatedly to plant a seed of inspiration, but he was convinced that he had nothing to gain from opening a book. One day when I again attempted to impress upon him the notion that reading could be beneficial, he pointed to a book on my shelf. "See that book?" he asked. "I can already tell you what it's about. Some kid who has a hard life and goes through some shit and overcomes it." He began pointing at other books, and continued, "And that's what *that* book's about, and *that* book, and *that* one. I don't want to read any of them."

Many urban charter schools that have emerged in recent years self-define with the mission to prepare students like Diego for college. Escenario identified as a college preparatory school and posted on its website the colleges that students in its graduating class would attend. Our charter network mission was to prepare 100% of students for admission into 2- or 4-year universities. Our college admissions data was the second most important factor in our funding, after our annual standardized test results.

In theory, Escenario directed college messaging to every student and required A-G courses—necessary for application and admission to the University of California and California State University systems—for graduation eligibility. The "College for All" message was designed to remedy an educational system that traditionally tracked students of color into classes that left them ineligible for four-year universities. Tracking developed in comprehensive public schools in the wake of *Mendez v. Westminister* and *Brown v. Board* to preserve in-school segregation when schools were forced to integrate (Bell, 2004; Oakes, 1985; Valencia, 2005). This is why many charter schools like Escenario attempt to "de-track" most or all of their academic classes (Oakes & Wells, 1998). UCSD's Preuss School, viewed as a model by many in the charter world, emphasizes de-tracking and a commitment to rigorous academic curriculum for underrepresented students (Alvarez & Mehan, 2006). Many charters focus on providing a college readiness curriculum to address the inequities that Ali and Jenkins observed in the early 2000s: "3 out of 4 African-American and nearly 4 out of 5 Latino graduates are not eligible for admission to the UC/CSU systems for lack of access to, and enrollment in an appropriate high school curriculum" (2002, p. 6). At Escenario, our AP courses were de-tracked and any student could theoretically participate. We required application to a 2- or 4-year university for students to receive a diploma.

On the surface, this sounds commendable. Yet the message intended to make higher education desirable and attainable for those who have historically been tracked out of college preparatory programs lacked school gravity for a student like Diego, who expressed his disdain for it. He was more compelled to pursue personal goals that were not aligned with our college mission: "Sky has a goal and as long as he reaches it, all the people that say he can't or shouldn't don't matter. . . . No he already knows what he wants and he will get it."

Some identifiable factors played into Diego's reasoning. One was his history of spotty relationships with previous teachers. Teacher transience in the charter and public school world had contributed to the inconsistencies he had seen with teachers coming and going, leaving mid-year, or having considerable trouble with teaching and managing students. Escenario was part of a charter management organization that relied on a pool of inexperienced teachers who were inexpensive to employ, many of whom came from the Teach for America program. My principal estimated that across our charter network, upwards of 50% of our teachers were Teach for America recruits in their first or second years of teaching. Many corporatized charters lean heavily on Teach for America, and this program meets a need by attracting teachers to work in challenging contexts where there are almost always teacher shortages. Yet TFA requires only one summer of preparation, and a 2-year commitment to teaching and professional growth in the field. In practice, some charter school networks place a revolving door of well-intended but inexperienced candidates—who may teach for 2 years before moving on to "real" jobs—in front of students who need teachers with pedagogical expertise and deeper awareness of the job (Darling-Hammond, 2010). Diego commented on this phenomenon in conversation with me, saying, "that's hella crazy when it's a cycle and you get like different teachers every year and you're barely connecting to one, or you're not connecting, and then go to another one and it's like *dang that's a year lost.*"

His argument ties to my experience as a teacher in a way that matters for this book. I applied to Teach for America after college and was rejected. So I went to a local school district and was hired to teach middle school at an arts-integrated, project-based K-8 school of choice. By the time I taught at Escenario and collected this data, I had been teaching middle and high school English and history, at both large comprehensive schools and small charter schools in urban districts, for 11 years. As a novice teacher, however, I did not have the pedagogical content knowledge (Shulman, 1986), the professional capacity, or the emotional maturity to conceptualize or execute the curriculum in this book. When I met Diego, Hazel, Abraham, Serenity, and the other students whose work and stories are included in this book, I had spent my adult life thinking deeply about what it meant to me and to them to be a White teacher in an urban context. Most or all of my students and their families had directly or indirectly been impacted by racism in a way that my family had not. Many critical race scholars speak to the increasing trend whereby urban public and charter schools employ a pool of predominantly White educators to prepare students of color for college and career success. Gloria Ladson-Billings writes, "The pervasiveness of whiteness makes the experience of most teachers an accepted norm. . . . The indictment is not against the teachers. It is against the kind of education they receive. The prospective teachers with whom I have worked generally express a sincere desire to work with 'all kinds of kids' . . . But where is the evidence that prospective teachers can get along with people different from themselves?" (2001, p. 81).

Christine Sleeter observes that in many teacher preparation programs, the majority of White candidates are receptive to learning about equity on a superficial level, and then enter the classroom and find themselves "completely unprepared for the students and the setting" (2001, p. 95). My principal at Escenario was clear with teachers that we were expected to spend our first year at the school (regardless of our experience) earning our students' trust. He was blunt in saying that this would be especially hard if we were White. He deliberately sought to hire teachers who saw it as their job to build mutual respect, rather than rely on positional power or demand compliance from students whose respect they struggled to earn. He told us that we could not succeed at Escenario if we were unable or unwilling to build relationships with the most challenging students.

My background was different from my students at Escenario for many reasons, one being the privileges that accompanied my race and social status. I grew up in a Southern town that did not start to desegregate until the mid-1970s. Mandatory busing began in Louisville the week that I was born, and mass protests were visible as my parents drove home from the hospital. My brother, who was in high school then, was sent by the same school that I would later attend to cover a Klan rally at a hotel not far from us for the school newspaper. The public schools placed most of my White classmates and me on the "advanced" track when we were in the second grade. The data that determined this placement were our standardized test scores from the first grade. Regardless of whether we were bused to a school in a White or Black neighborhood, we were kept together as a mostly White class, and we eventually had "top 3%" stamped on our diplomas when we graduated, as a final benefit of being on the highest track. There was little I needed to do to earn it. The system was structured in a way that worked clearly in my favor.

Despite how troubled my parents were, they both had college degrees because the doors of higher education were open to them in the 1940s when they graduated from high school. My father was the first in his family to attend college, and his education affected our economic class standing and our access to resources. All of my older siblings went to college, and four of us became teachers or professors. While my mother's illness took a toll on our finances in various ways, my father managed to hold things together on his income alone. He started drinking heavily when I was in middle school as his way of dealing with the situation, but he still went to work every day.

I had very few relationships with teachers in high school because I was too withdrawn and distrusting to connect to most adults. I had four older siblings, but they were much older than me and dealt with family conflict from a different place in life. At one point, I considered moving in with my brother, but I opted out of this idea when I realized that his wife was set against it. I lived with different friends at various points in high school. The instability in my home environment, and the self-loathing that I internalized from what I read as my mother's hatred of me, led me to check out emotionally. My school attendance was inconsistent, and I rarely went to a full day of classes. This was my attempt to control aspects of my life to make up for the general lack of control I felt. Nonetheless, I managed to keep my grades in the A and B range, with the exception of a few Cs. I also had a solid performing arts background. I studied dance at the local university and the district's performing arts magnet high school. This experience showed me that if I cared about something, then I could focus and eventually find my way.

I declared my college major in English, because I liked to read and write. Then I realized this landed me squarely in classes on English history and literature *only*. After struggling through multiple volumes of the Norton Anthology, I considered leaving college after my second year, because I felt disconnected and also ashamed of how academically underprepared I was. Around this time, a friend introduced me to ethnic studies classes, where I met a professor who reached out to me and took interest in me as a person. I did not have the awareness to question whether I was welcome in these classes when I started taking them. However, I spent my last 2 years in a learning environment that was unlike anything I had ever experienced in school, and by the end of college, I had a very different presence of mind. This was due in part to the readings and the professor, but more so to the life experiences and perspectives that I heard other students articulate.

I have reflected on why I was drawn to certain histories and personal stories, which became the catalyst for my reading and self-education and my ways of perceiving and engaging with the world since. Abuse did not happen to me in a social context, only a personal one. I think now that I wanted then to better understand the myriad ways that abuse impacts the human psyche and the struggles of people to dispel the negative messages that are forced on them. I was unable to explain to others the eccentricities of the world I had left or the despair of the adults in it, but I knew that I had normalized an experience that was not normal. Augusten Burroughs suggests in *Running with Scissors* (2002), a memoir of mental illness, that navigating normalcy is not an easy task after such a childhood. As I have mentioned previously, my comfort zone is an uncomfortable place, owing in part to my love template.

My experience with life struggle compelled me to reach out to a student like Diego, whose life was in many ways different from mine, but whose love template was similar. We had points of narrative intersection, and we had some candid conversations about them. Diego was the youngest child in his family by a long shot. I knew that he had tenuous relationships with both of his parents, and illness was present in his family. He lived with his older brother whom he idolized. It was an adequate living situation, except that Diego found his brother's girlfriend intolerable. She and Diego had disagreements, and he felt that she clearly did not want him around, so he eventually left his brother's house and moved in with a friend who was also my student. The irony was that Diego's story was, in some ways, my story. One of our interviews about his writing turned into a lengthy conversation about our families. He described how he had tried to make sense of the chaos in his life, and I could relate to his words, as he told me, "You don't know what the hell it is, you feel like *all these things are happening and I don't know why it's happening so I'm a victim of just my own ignorance kind of.*"

One reason why I was able to create school gravity for Diego in my class was because of the time we spent making these connections. Diego felt strongly that it was important for a teacher to meet students halfway. In his view, a teacher's hesitancy to be real with students created a sense of disconnect that prevented his or her classroom from working. He explained, "There are disconnections between teacher and student when the student gives fifty and the teacher gives below the fifty. But then there's vice versa, there's like the teacher going fifty and the student's not going fifty. . . . You gotta have patience, but patience is not gonna make him come to you, know what I mean?"

With regard to this point, he discussed two teachers he had known in high school. One was a teacher he sensed did not have a life struggle that allowed her to relate to some students. He also sensed that she actively knew this and made the effort to meet students where they were, which in turn made him want to engage. He described, "She's the one that got me thinking about how I can go fifty and someone else will go fifty and we finally connect between someone who didn't grow up the way I did, you know what I mean? . . . At first I was like *no, heck no, like I could never relate to someone who hasn't had struggle. . . .* But that's what I was planning to do with her. Push myself and push her too. I wanna find that connection." On the other hand, he described a teacher he felt had experienced real struggle in ways that she did not incorporate into her teaching. He explained, "But then that was the disconnect. . . . She didn't talk about it." He continued, "You know how you ask us to revise our essays and stuff? To get deeper meanings out of things. Like sometimes teachers just gotta revise the way they teach."

## THE ABSENCE OF AMBIGUITY: "YOU GET A'S OR YOU FAIL"

A second factor that influenced Diego's thinking about his life goals, and a reason why our school's college mission missed the mark with him, was because it did not target him as a thinker or learner in an authenticating way. Instead, the message felt imposed. He described, "It doesn't even allow like originality. Everybody's doing the same thing, getting tests the same way." His words raised the question as to how schools can provide an educational path that helps students express and explore their *own* identities and goals, rather than imposing these onto them.

Diego was sensitive to mixed messages that he perceived to promote higher learning under the guise of compliance. He was also distrustful of arbitrary definitions of success. He elaborated on this point in conversation with me, "I think that school sets for you just one success track and then the rest are failures, like *did this student follow the rules that we put for him? Like did this student follow the track that we put?* It's either you get the A's or you fail. It's either you try the assignments that you're given or you're just considered a non-educated person . . . and what I'm making it is not just for me to try to get the damn grade, what I'm making is so I could actually benefit, like I wanna use this outside."

Diego perceived a binary between "success" and "failure" that did not create space for where he fit as a student. Our educational system's practice of evaluation through these two categories is the focus of Hervé Varenne and Ray McDermott's (1998) book *Successful Failure—The School America Builds.* The authors contend that schools construct success in a way that is dependent on student failure, because the success of some students is interrelated to the failure of others. Both labels are limiting, because neither "can ever capture the good sense of what children can do" (p. 3). Varenne and McDermott argue, "We look at students officially identified as failing and we show them to be amazingly complex and ingenious in their responses to the pressures of their conditions" (p. 2). It is worth noting that Ray McDermott was one of my primary dissertation advisors, and his ideas were invaluable to the development of this work. When he first read about Diego, he immediately responded, "That's my kind of student." However, our charter network's view of success and failure did not allow ambiguity to see the value in Diego's life goals or outlook. Instead of revising these dual categories, our network reproduced them in a way that made him feel invisible.

Some colleagues and I have spent time looking at literature that captures different paradigms in the way that *academic identity* is treated in the research. Our college mission primarily targeted what my colleagues and I have referred to as *instrumental academic identity* (Wischnia, Nasir, LaMay, O'Connor, & Sullivan, 2010). We use the term *instrumental* to designate a view of school as the primary path to achievement. Research in this paradigm measures the extent to which students may appropriate and internalize the standard practices of school as relevant to their goals and self-esteem (Flores-Gonzales, 2002; Nasir, McLaughlin, & Jones, 2009; Pope, 2001; Steele, 1997). In contrast, we use the term *fundamental academic identity* to reference research that explores students' identities as learners rather than their internalization of traditional achievement measures. Research in this paradigm examines how students' development of academic identity may relate to authentic participation in classroom communities that promote real disciplinary work and encourage personal investment in learning (Boaler & Greeno, 2000; Lee, 2007; Reveles & Brown, 2008). In this context, students merge the work of self with the work of school in a way that is integral to their self- and world-perception. These conceptions of academic identity are not oppositional. Ideally, students would aspire to a healthy balance of authentic participation, good grades, meaningful learning, and a belief that school matters. In reality, the balance may tip depending on the student.

Given Diego's wary views of school, grades, and college, it could be easy to assume that he did not have an academic identity at all. Yet he found school gravity in thinking and learning in a way that eluded traditional measures of achievement. In order to rebuild his relationship with education, Diego needed to validate and foster his emerging fundamental academic identity, so he could then move toward a view of school as a means to an end that he wanted. To reach him, we first needed to appeal to his ways of thinking and to speak to his intellect and desire to learn. We needed to suspend the binaries of success and failure long enough to help him see and build connections between academic disciplines and his intuitions as a learner. Then, we needed to help him develop a stronger instrumental academic identity, which was our mission as a school. Instead, the "College for All" rhetoric imposed the view that college was the right path, without emphasizing the authentic learning experiences that a student like Diego needed as evidence. The message lacked school gravity because it circumvented who he was as a learner.

He captured his thinking on these issues in a story that he told me about his previous school:

> I remember in middle school I was talking to a math teacher and I was like *why the hell do we need this* and this was his straight up answer: *you need it to pass the damn test so you can graduate out of middle school and go to high school.* And I was like . . . fuck this. I was like *I don't really like school, you want me to do this so I can get into another school? This doesn't really apply to me.* And then I would keep thinking about things, like I would always ask questions like why, why would that add up to that. Why would I want a fraction of something, why wouldn't I just want the whole damn number? And then he never gave meaning to what I was doing, he was just like *cause you need fractions.* When I go home I don't really care how many slices of pie I eat, I just wanna eat the damn pie.

Over the course of our work, Diego continued to voice his frustration with the "College for All" message and why it overlooked his perspective as a learner. At the end of his junior year, he expressed, "People told me that, they were like *you can become anything you want,* and I was like *no I can't,* and now I realize I could. . . . When people tell you that you can do anything that you want, there's so much more explanation that goes into that . . . in a way that doesn't explain it to you but explains it to us."

## LOVE EQUALS STRUGGLE

In Diego's initial love narrative, struggle was a deterministic force. His writing had an angry, pessimistic tone and evoked the impression that desires and dreams were hard to attain. Like the educational system that he critiqued, his initial view of love lacked ambiguity. Diego did not feel able to fit into the school system's perception of who students should want to be. Yet he found himself stuck in a binary definition of "love" of his own making, which offered neither fulfillment nor hope.

A theme of conflict permeated Diego's initial love narrative, in which he portrayed relationships as a struggle between people who never align. He argued, "Why do people love the people that don't love them, and don't love the people that do love them? . . . In that case, why don't we all just be assholes? Then everyone will love you. Be the guy that people want but no one has. That would be fucking great. Except if you're not the asshole that everyone wants, you're the nice one that people walk over." If, as he argued, relationships are "push and pull all the time," then he questioned the point of even trying. If relationships are a set-up, then he reasoned that it makes sense to control the game. And if the game is one where someone inevitably wins and loses, then, he deduced, this should relieve us of some accountability.

Diego's reasoning connected to a larger point about struggle. When the odds seem stacked against us, then it is easier to justify a self-serving path. When life deals a raw deal, the least we can do is maintain our pride. We can adopt the defense of a disillusioned attitude toward a disappointing world. It is the veneer of Mike Rose's classmates in vocational education who "flaunt ignorance, materialize [their] dreams" (1989, p. 29), and it is the story of a hard knock life. While it may look like laziness, it is not, as Diego expressed to me in conversation: "But do you see where that ego would come from though? Like being told to do something and being through some shit just gets you to the point where you're like *no, fuck that I'm not gonna do what you want anymore, I'm gonna do me and I'm gonna make sure that everybody does what I want*. . . . I think it's just natural."

Diego predicated his initial narrative on his theory that *struggle = strength*. At a certain point, however, he began to trip over his own logic. If, as he argued, strong relationships necessitated struggle, which, in his equation, could not coexist with happiness, then it left him stuck in the paradox that the only way to grow stronger *was* to struggle, making it impossible to have a strong relationship that was also happy. Happy relationships, he concluded, were therefore illusory and had no legitimate place in the struggle. As Diego discovered, the triangulation between these concepts was tricky:

> Are complications in a relationship what makes two people
> grow stronger? Which does make sense. But if that's true, then
> happily-ever-after, of which my translation is smooth sailing, is far

from right. Happily-ever-after is arguing and arguing but growing and growing and if how much you're growing is worth all the arguing. This version doesn't sound as sweet as "as they lived happily ever after" because smooth sailing really means the two just don't care anymore enough to argue. So do you want smooth sailing, or do you want to argue?

Diego's initial narrative boiled down to an either-or equation in which happiness and struggle did not harmonize, and neither was satisfying on its own. The middle ground was missing. Relationships were either a struggle, or they were bogus; people either argued, or they ceased to grow; love was either smooth sailing, or it was turbulent. Living "happily ever after" was either deceptive, or it was euphemistic for "arguing and arguing but growing and growing and if how much you're growing is worth all the arguing."

There is no easy way, and there is little reward, because life is struggle.

## BREAKING TRADITION: LOVE + STRUGGLE = ENERGY

The accumulated rock of ages deciphered itself as a part of my inheritance—a part, mind you, not the totality—but, in order to claim my birthright, of which my inheritance was but a shadow, it was necessary to challenge and claim the rock. Otherwise, the rock claimed me.

—James Baldwin, *Notes of a Native Son*

As he tried to make deeper sense of his story, Diego began to explore through his writing a notion that we called *counterplot*. Counterplot is a story that gets *in* us when we don't know how it got there, and, without some kind of resolution, begins to take a life of its own.

Literary theorist Geoffrey Hartman (1958) defines plot and counterplot not as opposing narratives, but as storylines that create a kind of narrative incongruence. Counterplot's function is somewhat ambiguous, in that it works to contrast with the plot and to simultaneously parallel it. Plot and counterplot are *intertextual* (Bakhtin, 1981; Kristeva, 1980), meaning that they are made of multiple interwoven storylines that can coexist, collide, subsume, or counteract one another. The intertextuality between plot and counterplot can create the intermittent effect of crisis followed by narrative stasis, which leads the narrative in a direction that feels cyclical but fixed. Diego captured this dynamic in his second love narrative as he tried to identify a narrative template in his thinking: "I really don't know what to think about my own life, don't know why it seems like I'm always pulled into the same situations. Convinced that it can't be something someone's doing to me, but something I'm doing to myself." His description of family dynamics that appeared later in the paper conveyed his concern that his attempts to move forward were leading him backwards. It read:

> It's hard to see the story underneath your own. Most would like to say there isn't one, that there's no deeper reason why they do what they do, other than the obvious. It took me a while to realize why I found myself in the same situation so many times. There are so many stories buried underneath stories. Like a puppet master they manipulate us. It's often the things we do to prevent something from happening that let it happen.
>
> Everything I did to make sure I never turned out like my dad ended up being the source of why I'm so much like him. It's something that wasn't passed down by influence but something else that's much more harder to explain. Even though it seems to be easy for other people to see. For a while I think it was even hard for my mom to just look at me. You could see the pain in her eyes more and more each day as she was realizing how much I was like him. At such a young age of course I was confused why my mom was so distant, but still it didn't bother me as much as it does now. So now I find myself abandoned in a stranger's shoes with no clue in what direction to go.

Diego became increasingly motivated to understand the "something else that's much harder to explain" that he identified in his writing. Over his next several papers, he began to look into the idea that he could break cycles of what he called "tradition" and convert life struggle into a positive rather than a deterministic force. His writing began to display more ambiguity as he moved toward a stance of inquiry in his outlook on love and life. The shifts in his definition of love that became apparent in his personal and academic writing eventually transferred to his view of the educational system and his understanding of what it could offer.

Diego also recognized some of the limitations that his earlier thinking had imposed on his story. In conversation with me, he reflected on his initial love narrative, "Like in my first love paper I had an *it's pointless* tone and now I think I mean it more like a question of, *if people can see that it's probably not going to work why do they still try and make it work?* On that note, now I'm thinking of a counterargument of *why shouldn't we try and have love where there is no love?* And on the whole 'smooth sailing' thing . . . I need that healthy friction but there is a thin line between that and hurtful and damaging, scarring friction. That could have been a good paper right there."

*   *   *

As Diego probed what he perceived as his counterplot, he initially had trouble with the idea that one could succeed at "breaking tradition," as he put it. His operative metaphor for his narrative template was that struggle creates "dents in our frame." This is where his essential question emerged: *Do we shape our stories or do our stories shape us?* In his second love narrative, he wrote:

> Branches that shape my hands are reaching for my own unknown path, but the seed I came from, that developed into the twisted, unstable, inherited rituals that were undetected but still injected in my head, have already been growing roots for so long on my past actions that it almost seems pointless to break tradition.

As Diego thought more about his future direction, he began to question whether his inclination toward the armed services transpired from his counterplot. He decided that the tenor of his life experience could predispose someone to self-select into a no-win position. I found the following lines in one of his in-class assignments: "It's sad, but a fucked up counterplot is a great recipe for what could be an amazing soldier. We are trained with the mentality of making something out of nothing. Are the people that are in the armed forces mostly people that know struggle?"

Diego's narrative work led him to a new theory that became central to his thinking: We convert struggle into fuel. The type of fuel is up to us. This revision to his outlook was pivotal, because it was the first time that he acknowledged his struggle as a positive shaping force, or acknowledged his agency to shape the outcome.

This shift emerged in his academic writing in his analysis of Toni Morrison's character, Guitar. He chose to examine Guitar in light of Malcolm X, in part because he was reading a book on Malcolm X for his Spanish class at the same time that he was writing his paper. While there were similarities in these two men's stories, he argued that the main difference between them was how they convert their life stories into fuel.

In the novel, Guitar deals with excruciating loss in childhood when his father is killed, then his mother disappears, and he is passed from one family member to another. Guitar expresses, "Everything I ever loved in my life left me" (p. 307). As an adult, he becomes a member of an organization called the Seven Days. The setting is around the time of Emmett Till. Guitar is the Sunday man, which means that whenever Whites murder Blacks on a Sunday, his mission is to kill Whites in the same manner on the same day of the week. Guitar operates on a narrative that becomes increasingly dualistic as the novel progresses. In his paper, Diego interpreted, "Guitar's love for his people evaporated out from the loss of his father. . . . You can imagine where feeling like he had to defend his people came from, knowing that his father was murdered. Guitar is the real deal, avenger at full scale, but loses himself in the process and now can't trail his way back."

Diego argued that Guitar's story shaped him rather than the other way around, because he fell into the mindset of justifying actions that were understandable in the context. Diego also asserted that Guitar's ability to rationalize his choices did not make them positive, because it was his responsibility to "break tradition" even when he could justify the opposite. He explained, " . . . if that energy was helped to be channeled, the possibilities for the positive and constructive actions [Guitar] could have made would have been limitless. He might even have been able to fly."

This point became the crux on which Diego's thinking began to turn, and it was the moment when his relationship with school began to change direction. Diego tied his argument about Guitar to his own justification of his outlook on school and life. He knew that he could easily justify the position that he took in "Sky's Plan," given his experience and his struggle. Yet he began to question whether he was unconsciously allowing an oppressive system to shape him. He explained, "I could easily use the unnecessary struggle I have as an excuse for why I don't want to do something. What a waste that would be. At times I do cover up my laziness with legit reasoning, like Guitar covers his revenge with the legit love for his people, but that doesn't make either of our actions positive."

Diego realized a key point of school gravity at this point in his work: Different disciplines connect. He began to notice how different disciplines attempted to address issues in the world in complementary ways, and this inspired him to try to synthesize and apply material he encountered in different academic classes to questions he cared about. His insight into interdisciplinary connection explains the scientific undertone of the term *school gravity*. Diego's final papers built on parallels that he drew between momentum and energy, concepts that he discussed in his physics class, to his counterplot and a story of struggle. Through scientific metaphor, he reworked the *love = struggle* equation from his initial love narrative to assert that *love + struggle = energy*. Similarly, his definition of love evolved from "something you hope is there but never is," to "some sort of energy . . . an energy that can never be destroyed, only transferred."

He also shifted from seeing what he *lacked* to what he *had*. In his final academic essay, he argued, "Love is energy if it's given or not given . . . not knowing what you want is often a sign of just not knowing what you have." The law of thermodynamics states that energy is neither created nor destroyed as it changes form, and Diego decided that love and counterplot have similar properties. They cannot be created or destroyed, but they *can* change form, depending on the quality of momentum into which someone chooses to convert personal and social struggle. The problem arises when we don't see or determine the form this conversion takes.

Diego increasingly began to look for what he interpreted as common storylines in his different academic classes, and he creatively located them between his literary analysis, his self-narrative, and his understanding of scientific concepts. In conversation with me, he explained, "You can connect things just daily. You can connect templates, storylines, it's all connected, it's just part of life." When I asked him to verbalize the changes in his thinking over the course of 10th and 11th grade, he told me:

> The connect is the biggest thing I got, like you could connect the way you use certain different examples. Life is just a big scramble of connections, and you just gotta find, if you think you don't relate to someone you're hella wrong. If you think things don't relate then you're hella wrong. If you think things happen for no reason then you're hella wrong 'cause things do happen for a reason and . . . to find the connections you gotta find the storyline behind it, you gotta find the why things happen.

Diego realized that he could, in fact, learn from almost anything if he could connect the "why things happen" to something that he perceived in the world that mattered.

Self-affirmation and inquiry began to displace some of Diego's previous defenses. This was evident in the final lines of his final paper: "Instead of I can't, now I can, I should, and I am . . . the previous *I don't knows* and *I don't cares* are now *I do care and I could find out*."

## "EDUCATIONAL REFLEXES": THE RELEVANCE OF PAULO FREIRE AND ACADEMIC CITATIONS

Diego's writing embodied the identity work that allowed him to find points of connection to school, and his engagement with education changed as a result. He was no longer a kid who refused to read; instead, he became a student who wanted to tease apart his love of thinking and learning from the tedium of school. He began to see education as something that potentially offered answers connected to real struggle.

Toward the end of his junior year, Diego became one of a group of students who started to hang around after school for a couple of hours every day. Sometimes he and his friends would just mess around. Other times, he would engage his teachers in conversations about social and educational issues. One of my colleagues began taking Diego and a small group of his friends to teacher workshops on social justice, which were a catalyst for Diego to think more about school macro-narratives and structures. I was grading papers after school in my room one afternoon when I heard Diego track down my colleague to talk about something that was on his mind. He asked him into my room to listen to some thoughts that he was struggling to resolve about the purpose of education. The two began a passionate dialogue about whether the purpose of school was to maintain or overturn the status quo and whether both purposes could exist simultaneously. The conversation grew to the point where several other students and teachers overheard it and came into the room. As the discussion continued, my board quickly became covered with diagrams and labels, as an informal debate erupted around questions of wealth and poverty, social status and social problems, and the impact of education in remedying social inequity or maintaining it.

Educational issues increasingly became one of Diego's favorite topics, and, unlike most of my students, he began to seek me out to discuss his ideas for how curriculum could connect to life and how we could help students experience satisfaction and peace of mind through education. Diego told me in a conversation at the end of the year that he had searched online and discovered a website where he could read quotations from Freire. I only knew about this because he mentioned it offhand. He interrupted me after something I said and replied, "Oh, Paulo Freire said something about that. He said like *if you don't have a real source of identity then you don't have a real source of struggle.*" I immediately asked him, "Where did Paulo Freire say that?" and the rest of our dialogue went as follows:

> *Diego:* He said that, like you could pick it up right now, like I kind of read his stuff like that.
> *Ms. LaMay:* Wait wait wait. Where did you look him up, where did you find this?
> *Diego:* You can find quotes by him on the Internet.
> *Ms. LaMay:* Okay. So you've looked up Freire quotes online.
> *Diego:* Yeah.
> *Ms. LaMay:* On your own.
> *Diego:* Yeah.
> *Ms. LaMay:* That's pretty cool.
> *Diego:* 'Cause Freire's pretty cool.

As Diego began to form what were essentially his own educational philosophies, he began to question everything. He wanted to understand what Standard English was, who set the "standard," and why it was privileged. He wanted to know who decided what curriculum was taught in each grade level and why people who made policy decisions were disconnected from the classroom. He wondered where MLA citations came from, and, not surprisingly, he argued with academic conventions in general.

One of our conversations included a lengthy digression about the purpose of quotations in academic writing. Over the 2 years that we worked together, I had a hard time getting him to use quotations. There were few of them in his academic essays, because, as a matter of principle, he did not want to include someone else's words if someone told him to. He also felt that quotations broke the flow of his thoughts. Any argument I made about academic conventions went nowhere with him, unless I could show him why the conventions had a real purpose. So I opened a dissertation that a former doctoral candidate had shared with me, and I pointed out to him how the author had provided citations that the reader could use to track down what certain other writers had said. For the first time, Diego was able to see how quotations were actually helpful if he was trying to use someone's paper as a source of information. He immediately told me that my students would have grasped the purpose of the convention better if I had created a lesson where they were using the information in parentheses for a purpose that felt real to them. He suggested that I could create a kind of scavenger hunt and ask students to look in the parenthesis for the clues, so they could experience what it was like to actually *use* the citations to find things they were looking for.

This conversation marked an important moment. Diego had found a way to engage with the scholarly community on its terms as well as his. This was a palatable compromise for him, and as he mentally designed a way to teach citation, he thought like a teacher and student at once. His teacher mind considered how to effectively communicate to his student mind the relevance of the citations that he had just learned to appreciate.

Over Diego's senior year, he decided that he wanted to apply to college and potentially engage in the educational struggle—in other words, teach. He applied and received acceptance from two schools. One was a state university, and the other was a local private college with a program geared to prepare students of color from local public school districts to teach in their own communities. The introduction to his personal statement included a Freire quote that he researched and found on his own:

> "Education . . . becomes the practice of freedom, the means by which men and women deal critically and creatively with reality and discover how to participate in the transformation of their world." Paulo Freire's definition of education is relevant to many students' school experiences, including mine. Students can go from feeling as if school is pointless to understanding the point of education; I am proof of that. To me, education is about giving value to knowledge, and helping students find a passion in learning through bridging the disconnect between homeroom and home. Teaching is most valuable when it shows students how to use school material to break down life obstacles. In my opinion, a teacher's most important job is to connect school to students' daily lives and help them use the connection as a tactic to spark a deeper understanding of the world around them. When my teachers took this approach to me, my views really began to be challenged, and they would have been ignored if not for a teacher. I want to be that teacher for the generation to come and generations after.

Diego, who is pictured in Figure 6.1, felt strongly that school should place more emphasis on helping young people self-educate and giving them a reason why they should want to. In a piece he wrote voluntarily and shared with several of his teachers, he explained, "It took me about 3 years to come to the conclusion of *even if the material teachers use to teach me doesn't affect my*

**Figure 6.1. "If you're using education constantly outside and inside, then it becomes valuable, it becomes useful, it becomes something that sets you free."**

*life directly, gaining the skills of knowing how to get the answers and gaining educational reflexes will.*" Educational reflexes, he argued, connected to Freire's definition of what education is supposed to be. He described, "When I read Freire, it's like down to earth, like *dude use what you got, learn what you got, and you connect it to real life shit, you use it day to day* . . . and Paulo Freire talks about that too, he talks about how you should use education as an instrument. And like, by my definition if you have an instrument then you're using it constantly. If you're using your education constantly outside and inside, then it becomes valuable, it becomes useful, it becomes something that sets you free."

# The School Gravity of Love

**Education:** *noun.* Not the knowledge itself but the knowledge of how to practice that knowledge.

—Diego's Definition

I am still in contact with the students whose writing appears in this book. Social media is helpful for this. Since this project originated as a dissertation and evolved into a publication, I have sent drafts of these chapters to the students in them and asked for their thoughts, feedback, approval, and response. In addition to ongoing conversations, baby showers, and reunion meals with students and staff who were at Escenario, I have tried to maintain a relationship with them through writing over the time that has passed.

When *Writing Love and Agency* was in the dissertation stage, I sent a draft of Diego's chapter to him so he could read it and share his thoughts. I also sent it to my graduate school advisor, Andrea Lunsford, who supported and advised this work from the time when I could not yet articulate what it was. I thought it could be interesting to send the email to them both, so I added them together as recipients. I was pleasantly surprised later to check my inbox and read that Diego and Andrea had struck up an email conversation on the topic of struggle. As the email continued, their exchange evolved into dialogue about how school knowledge can and should connect to its real-world purpose.

Diego's initial email included an answer to both Andrea and me, in response to a question I had posed about how he would define the theme of his five papers over the curriculum. He wrote: "If I would have to give you a theme for my papers, something you can follow through all of them is how life is really what you make it. And you can't let struggles keep you from achieving. Because you can be proud of those struggles, but first you have to overcome them, and to overcome them first you have to stop saying why me." What struck me about his language—with the exception of "why me" at the end—was how similar it was to the rhetoric of schooling that promotes achievement by overcoming the odds and reaching our dreams. This was not an outlook that he had appropriated from a poster on a classroom wall or from messages in our charter network brochure. Diego had arrived

116

at these lines and found some truth in them through his own journey. The words meant something to him, and the concept of "struggle" was central to the iterations of his argument about whether we shape our stories or the other way around. He had developed a level of respect for education through meaningful experiences with it.

Andrea Lunsford is a teacher in the truest sense, and she took Diego's invitation to engage as an opportunity to respond. Her message to him read as follows:

Dear Diego:
Thanks for copying me on this message to Ms. LaMay. I really hear what you are saying about the ongoing nature of struggles: I am still finding that I have struggles to make and things to overcome. But I can also say that it has gotten a lot easier over the years as I have learned how to control my responses to things that happen. A lot easier.
I hope I get to meet you soon!
Best wishes,
Andrea

Diego had then responded:

I think it's great that you admit to still having struggle because it shows that you are still growing as a person and reaching even higher levels of understanding. There's a lot of strength that comes from that. There are a lot more important things to learn from in the process of overcoming struggle, that I think school never covers. I also think that that's partly the student's responsibility to connect the text to world and I'm glad that I was introduced to that . . . It's also frustrating to think that I'm just realizing how a text could really have a positive impact in my world. I feel like one of the first things you should learn at school is not the knowledge itself but the knowledge of how to practice that knowledge because I feel like so much is forgotten if not used and proven of its importance in life, so students could really understand the value of education.

And finally, Andrea wrote:

Dear Diego:
What you say about it's "not the knowledge itself but the knowledge of how to practice that knowledge" is absolutely right—and very profound. You are thinking in such strong, positive ways; no wonder Ms. LaMay is so impressed with your work!
What are you doing this summer? I am writing every day—revising two textbooks I have written—and though it is in a way hard

work, I like it because it feels like an accomplishment and it gives a structure to my days. (I am taking some time off, though, to take long walks along the ocean and also to visit friends!)

Sending best wishes,

Andrea

The exchange ended there. However, I still agree with Andrea that Diego's words are significant: "I feel like one of the first things you should learn at school is not the knowledge itself but the knowledge of how to practice that knowledge." This book exists because Diego, Hazel, Abraham, Kylie, and all of the students in it were willing to share their work with a wider audience in the spirit with which Abraham shared his story with our class—so that others could learn from it. My desire to publish their writing, and their individual and shared stories, connects to their desire to practice their knowledge in a way that can potentially bear on the educational experiences of young people who struggle to find school relevant. Luis Rodriguez, in *Hearts and Hands— Creating Community in Violent Times*, writes, "For many of the youth I've worked with, being clear about the role of the system in their lives and their capacity to contribute to change in that system is a major part in helping them to become the strong, caring, and transcendent people we want to claim" (2001, p 197). To find agency through school, many young people need to feel like a partner in their educational process, so it feels as though school is doing things *with* them rather than *to* them. It is my students' hope and mine that their experiences and views, and their willingness to voice them in this book, can have a possible influence beyond themselves and help to bring school gravity for students who have not had sufficient positive experiences with school to make education a desirable goal.

## THE LANGUAGE OF CORPORATE EDUCATION REFORM: "WORDS WITH NO SHADOWS"

When I was at Escenario, our administrative and teaching staff was oriented toward social justice in a way that the larger charter network was not. The school no longer exists as it did, because the educators that I knew there have since moved on to contexts where we felt better aligned. Several of us still work together. In a speech he gave several years ago, Bill Ayers (2006) argued that "school is always a contested space: what should be taught? In what way? Toward what end? By and for whom? At bottom, it involves a struggle over the essential questions: what does it mean to be a human being living in a human society?" These kinds of questions surfaced then in our school and charter network, just as they continue to emerge now in debate that includes a continuum of corporate-minded educators and those with a deeper vision of social justice.

Another person whose vision of education and creative administrative tactics made the context for this research feasible was my school principal, Larry Vilaubi, who has also assisted in reading many of these chapters. He structured our English department in such a way to let me work with the students in this book for 2 consecutive years, and then he kindly and supportively got out of my way. This 2-year time frame allowed my students and me to build the relationships that were essential to make any of this work. However, it was to my principal's credit that our second year was able to happen. At the end of our first year, the CEO of our network appealed to him to let me go because she did not feel my students' test scores were high enough. My principal decided differently, and as I mentioned at the start of this book, my students' scores rose significantly in the spring of their junior year and boosted our Annual Yearly Progress measure over 80 points. This was not because I narrowed my teaching to the test, although strategies for doing so were the primary focus of professional development at our charter network teacher meetings. As I mentioned in the beginning, I believe my students chose to engage with the test differently because they had more academic confidence, and they were more aware of the game they were playing to qualify their achievement and mine. Their depth of learning and engagement that they demonstrate in the thinking and writing that appear throughout this book could never be captured by a standardized test. Nevertheless, the most effective way to raise the achievement of students whose school associations are negative is to humanize their learning experience. This is why a key premise of this book is the contention that teaching for social-emotional and academic engagement in a way that *rebuilds students' relationships with school* is both realistic and needed in the current political and educational climate. School gravity and student achievement go hand in hand.

Many charter schools began as part of a progressive reform movement. Before momentum shifted to the current corporatization of charter and public schools, Larry Cuban (2004) anatomized the business model implicit in the practice of standardization in *The Blackboard and the Bottom Line: Why Schools Can't Be Businesses*. It includes the development of rigorous academic standards for all students, which are taught through scripted textbooks and assessed through frequent standardized tests. Schools are rewarded or punished according to this narrow measure of achievement and success. Joel Westheimer recently described the current standardized movement as an "unprecedented time . . . what used to be the broad purposes of education have been narrowed to a myopic focus on so-called standards and accountability in only two subject areas—math and literacy—and then even within those . . . only the most narrow and emaciated conception of what those areas have to offer" (Yale, 2015). This has created what Diane Ravitch, who formerly supported charter schools and No Child Left Behind, now calls a "forced academic march" in conditions that treat students as though they learn identically and their identities, dreams, and realities are irrelevant to the learning process (Yale, 2015).

This standardized approach contrasts sharply with the work I present in this book, which seeks to differentiate writing and revision to engage students in learning that works best for them, by respecting their individual strengths, stories, and struggles and situating their work in an educational community of caring teachers and peers where they could engage deeply. Patrick Camangian notes that the idea of standards is not a problem as much as the fact that "we haven't treated children as the subjects of their own studies. We haven't used young people's lives as a starting place of all learning" (Yale, 2015). Many public and charter schools claim that their mission is to prepare students for college and careers. Yet they compromise this mission by disregarding their students' fundamental human needs. He explains, "When you look at Common Core . . . it still under narrates how young people could heal from a lot of the self-hate that comes from their cultures being excluded from the curriculums that are being imposed on them. It doesn't talk about the skill of developing knowledge of self. It doesn't talk about the skill of developing self love" (Yale, 2015).

My students intuitively pushed back on this form of hypocrisy. Toni Morrison describes certain characters in her novels, including Guitar, whose alienation and anger drew my students' respect, as those whose determination to express "either an effort of the will or a freedom of the will" is misunderstood (Taylor-Guthrie, 1994, p. 165). She clarifies that "it's not about meanness. It's a kind of self-flagellant resistance to certain kinds of control, which is fascinating" (p. 165). Her description fits the defenses that many of my students developed to shield themselves from hostile school environments. In some cases, their resistance took the form of what Herbert Kohl (1991) calls "willed not learning," which can be mistaken for failure to learn (p. 10). "Willed not learning" occurs in educational conditions where power and authority are enacted over students in ways that make school gravity impossible. Kohl explains, "To agree to learn from a stranger who does not respect your integrity causes a major loss of self. The only alternative is to not-learn and reject the stranger's world" (p. 16).

In the introduction to this book, Serenity described her writing and its connection to herself as "words that had shadows." As she spoke of her development as a writer, she expressed, "Now . . . there's something behind them. Before, they were like freakin' pieces of string with nothing, like thin air, like they weren't even really there." Her metaphor describes what I observed in my students' responses to shallow educational rhetoric. They had trouble with the false pretense of equity in the language of the educational system, which, to them, was like "pieces of string with nothing, like thin air."

Ken Yale recently produced a public radio series called "The Battle for Public Education in the 21st Century." He argues that the seeds of the current movement for corporatized education originated in the 1980s, as right wing movements organized against the gains won by civil rights and liberation movements in the 1960s and 1970s that pushed for educational reforms like desegregated, equitable schools and multicultural curriculum. Over recent years, Yale argues that corporate education privatizers have grown more sophisticated in their skill at coopting the language of progressive educational reform. In other words, an average person listening to a debate about school policy could have trouble distinguishing between those who want a more socially just public school system, and those who want to shut down public education and replace it with a privately owned and operated system. Everyone speaks of equity and accountability and centers this argument on "underprivileged youth"—mostly low-income students of color—with the plea that our schools cannot let them fail. But demanding that public schools demonstrate accountability by raising standardized test scores, without providing the necessary funding and proper support, or addressing the systemic poverty and oppression of students and their communities, guarantees that many schools will fail. This then becomes a rationale to close public schools and corporatize their replacement with the formula described in Cuban's earlier assessment. Yale explains:

> The most powerful men and women behind the curtain . . . have coopted and mastered the language of progressive educational reform. It's often hard to tell who is really speaking. They've enlisted an army of think tanks, politicians, public relations firms, and corporate media to sell their message. It's all about leaving no child behind, certainly not about opening up a trillion dollar education market for corporate profit. Those behind the curtain tap into legitimate criticisms of educational inequity and public school failure. This is fertile ground to reshape public education in their corporatized image.

This misappropriation of the language of equity and access tied to the distrust that I observed in Diego's response to our school's college mission. It was tough for him to read the motive. Why would a charter school network promote higher education through scripted curriculum that emphasized testing? Was he being taught how to think or how to comply? Was the goal to offer him a path to educational access that many middle-class, White students take for granted, or was the goal to impose values and norms that were Eurocentric, corporate, colonial, and hegemonic? His perception of conflicting paradigms was accurate. At times, the goal appeared to be both.

## A PLACE WHERE THE LOVE IS "GENEROUS"

The four necessary human relationships: to love; to be loved; to be a teacher; to be a pupil.

—W. H. Auden

As I was writing this final chapter, I sent it to Diego and asked if he wanted to contribute. He did, and part of his response read:

> I remember my exact train of thought for most of what you mentioned, and my mentality hasn't changed much. Although I like to think I've grown quite a bit since high school, a lot has carried onto the later chapters of my life. I still try and find ways to make things work on my terms because I like to have control of my life. It's a big part of what makes me, me. I was someone who felt as if things were happening to him, instead of because of him. . . . I felt like all my effort was directed to goals that were never discussed with me. I challenged the assignments, I challenged the reading material. I didn't want to take another step without someone telling me why. Looking back I still feel like I had reason to feel the way I did. At least when I denied the good intentions of my teacher it was my decision, I made that choice for myself.
>
> It really drains your morale or "school gravity" when you don't know why you're doing what you're doing. No one is more hard working than a person with purpose. Can you imagine a student coming into class on a mission? . . . It can be as simple as making a student feel special.

Diego is the assistant narrator for this book because he invariably voiced one of its primary points: We can humanize students by listening to their ways of thinking, writing, knowing, and understanding that are not incorporated into our educational system but are essential to their sense of mission and purpose.

My students found school gravity in their realizations about school, writing, love, themselves, one another, and the ways that these could connect through one another's writing and narrative revisions. The school gravity of love dealt with the realness of their lives, which may seem peripheral in a systemic context but was central to their growth. Without this angle on learning, I am not sure how we reach Kylie. I am not sure how we convince Sofia to want to attempt an assignment. I am not sure how we push Abraham to focus his mind on academic content, if he has to deny or avoid what blocks him from positive participation. I am not sure how we help Hazel see the connections between her writing outside of class to the moment "when Milkman goes to Danville . . . that's where I think I'm connecting with my academic paper." If we do not relate education to our students as people, I am not sure how, in Patrick's words, we get them to see how "you grow academically off your past experiences." Without emphasizing the connections between personal and academic perception, I am not sure how we reach Diego and help him to see that "life is just a big scramble of connections . . . if you think things don't relate then you're hella wrong." In education, as in life, there are no magical transformations. If we engage honestly with the minds of youth, then this means dealing on a real level with their "actual language . . . anxieties, fears, demands, dreams," and with the intricacies of the ways they think (Freire, 1987, p. 6).

These intricacies of thinking emerged in an impassioned conversation that I caught one afternoon toward the end of the school year. It mixed wisdom, confusion, and tears. It involved Hazel, Patrick, Serenity, and a student named Jose. It began as a dialogue about grades. The students were debating the importance of "the paper" versus the value of their life experience before it turned to the core of the issue: self-love.

Patrick had drawn a diagram on the board with the word "You" circled in the middle. Above the circle he had written the words "Do Need Coll"—which translated to "we do need college"—and below the circle he had written "Fuck it." When I arrived to the conversation, they were arguing about why they spent so much time stuck in the latter mindset.

Patrick was saying:

A lot of students stay in this mode where they're like *fuck it, I don't see any meaning to school*, and the way [teachers] try to structure it is how we get from here (pointing to "Fuck it") to here (pointing to "Do Need Coll"). That's how some of us are seeing it, like *this is shit, we don't need this*. But the fact is that we need to get these grades higher because it's going to matter in the long run.

Patrick was talking partly about his own grades, but the reference to "these grades" was to Serenity's grades that she had written on the board and was debating with Hazel and Jose about in Figure 7.1. They included a D and F. Then Hazel pointed to them and argued, "Why do they have to put a letter on how we are when they *see* how we are already? I mean, we're not just an A, B, C, but we *are*, and they know us by our name but they're still labeling us, and if we get an F, that labels us failure. Why do they have to label us when they see our potential every day?" As the debate continued, my students kept referring to Serenity's grades as "the paper." Jose expressed, "There's a lot of people who know how to get grades, but don't know how to do stuff with other people. They're going to get the paper, but they don't have the experience in their own lives."

Diego's words earlier in this chapter echo the sentiments that many of my students held, especially their resentment at feeling defined by terms that devalued their experience. The four students who stayed in my classroom to debate this topic described an intense conflict between the pressure to take a college path that they knew on one level was important and their anger at a system that felt oppressive. As Diego reflected, "At least when I denied the good intentions of my teacher it was my decision, I made that choice for

**Figure 7.1. (From Left to Right) Jose, Hazel, and Serenity Debate "The Paper" Versus Life Experience**

myself." At the time, Hazel also identified this tension as the main issue: "We already cracked the argument that we all know what we need to do to get to college and we all know that we're right here with *fuck it.* . . . We don't want to move up but we want to be up."

At this point, Patrick said, "I think we're stuck here, we're too comfortable here, we're scared to go to the top."

This conversation exemplified how my students struggled to reframe their relationships with school. They were trying to balance their view that school felt like an imposition, and, in Diego's words, like "goals that were never discussed with me," with something that was *theirs.* They were also trying to resolve the problem of their dependency for advancement on a system that made their lives feel inconsequential. Essentially, they were trying to switch their perspectives on the issue without dismissing those they held, which was evident in the flip-flopping of their arguments. The irony in the conversation was that someone would start to argue how they should all learn to succeed without making excuses and then get interrupted by a peer who pointed out that this was a simplistic critique of the ways they *all* contradicted themselves. An example was this exchange between Hazel and Serenity:

> *Serenity:* This paper is what they're going to judge us on. They don't judge us on our experience.
> *Hazel:* That's the point.
> *Serenity:* But you guys are not doing nothing, you're keeping the grades *here* (pointing to "the paper").
> *Hazel:* But you can't exclude yourself from that! We need *this* (points to "the paper") to get to *there* (points to "Do Coll Now"). Your

grades won't get us there ("Do Coll Now"). They get us *there* ("Fuck it").

*Serenity:* But don't we all have experience? And our grades are what we have to show for it. Everyone's saying *what do we need school for, fuck school, fuck the grades, I have all this experience.* But this paper is your way of showing.

*Hazel:* Listen! I love you to death but this is *your grades* (pointing to "the paper").

*Serenity:* Exactly!

*Hazel:* So why are these your grades?

*Serenity:* Cause I don't think I need all of this in the future.

*Hazel:* So what is your argument? You're arguing about *yourself!*

*Serenity:* Yes I am, and this is the point of this, I use this as an excuse to say *why the hell am I gonna need this in the future?* What is math, what is history, what is all this gonna do to my future if I have all this experience? Why do I need these letter grades? And that's what I'm fighting myself on.

*Hazel:* Yeah that's what we're all fighting ourselves on.

*Serenity:* But notice how you're fighting yourself that you do need the paper.

David Johnson and Roger Johnson (2004) maintain that one of the most important social-emotional competencies for life happiness is *self-actualization,* or the extent to which we know our talents and abilities and can apply them. They define self-actualization as "the drive to actualize potential and take joy and a sense of fulfillment from being all that a person can be" (p. 41). In this moment, I had stumbled onto a conversation that showed me just how deeply my students struggled with a fundamental problem: Despite the positive moments that I observed in many of their experiences at Escenario, their agency to self-actualize felt compromised by a system that was never originally designed for their empowerment. So they sought agency elsewhere, while trying to hang onto the hope that they could make their education somehow meaningful. It was around this point when the topic of love entered the conversation. Hazel took it in this direction when she said, "I come to school because of the love I get."

Love was the strongest school gravity factor that I witnessed in the 2 years I spent working with the students whose voices fill this book. Toni Morrison illuminates the need to "get to a place where the love is generous" (Taylor-Guthrie, 1994, p. 171), and this phrase is relevant to their experiences with education. In *Teaching the Taboo,* Rick and William Ayers draw attention to a fundamental problem with the word *teaching,* as they explain, "*Teaching* . . . the trouble starts right here with the suggestion of a 'giver' and a 'receiver'" (p. xv). Gregory Boyle (2010) also reminds us that compassion is a "covenant between equals," not a relationship between the healer and the wounded. A generous love is grounded in common struggle and common humanity, and this quality is, in Diego's words, what could "make a student feel special."

As the debate that I observed came to a close that afternoon, Serenity began to talk about a relationship in her life that "is not coming back—ever—and I know that now, so why am I gonna let that stop me? I don't want people to look at me and say *she can't do it because of what she's been through*. You can't let that stop you from where you know you want to be. You want to not struggle in life." Then Hazel spoke openly of the loneliness that came with trying to maintain this view. She expressed, "I don't want to be alone. I get so scared when I'm alone. How do I get to the point where I'm not scared to be alone?"

Toward the end of the year, Serenity conveyed an important understanding about a lesson she had pulled from the novel we had read. She had explained to me, "And then it didn't get better, I mean his parents didn't fall in love all over again . . . and Hagar didn't live and move on from Milkman, and Ruth didn't, you know, figure out her problems, it was like a love that was missing . . . so everything basically just stayed the same, except Milkman knew where he stood." This description was one that also fit many of my students. The work that they did was hard, and, in many cases, the struggles in their lives did not cease. In the end, they knew better where they stood.

To take a different kind of agency in our lives, we have to love ourselves enough to confront our stories. The biggest question we may face as educators is how to create educational spaces where young people can find a love that is generous. As Hazel wrote in her definition, "We're broken little pieces playing games with ourselves . . . the love's there, it might be hard to find, but it's one thing that can keep us together. One love."

# Notes

## Chapter 1

1. *Joker One* was a book I had brought to show Diego after a post-class discussion when he had insisted I couldn't change his mind about reading. This memoir, written by Princeton graduate and U.S. Marine Donovan Campbell, was a vivid account of his platoon's eight-month deployment in Ramadi, Iraq. Diego had skimmed through only through the first two pages, but had walked away with my copy of the book.

## Chapter 4

1. Hazel later gave me her handwritten copy of this poem and asked if I would type it and give it back to her. The version that she gave me is the version I have presented.

# References

Ali, R., & Jenkins, G. (2002). *The high school diploma: Making it more than an empty promise*. Oakland, CA: Education Trust West.

Alvarez, D., & Mehan, B. (2006). Whole-school detracking: A strategy for equity and excellence. *Theory Into Practice, 45*(1), 82–89.

American Psychiatric Association. (1994). *Diagnostic and statistical manual of mental disorders* (4th ed.). Washington, DC: Author.

Ayers, R., & Ayers, W. (2014). *Teaching the taboo: Courage and imagination in the classroom*. New York, NY: Teachers College Press.

Ayers, W. (2006, November). Bill Ayers: World Education Forum. Retrieved from billayers.org/2006/11/

Bakhtin, M. (1981). *The dialogic imagination*. Austin: University of Texas Press.

Bazerman, C. (2004). Intertextualities. In A. F. Ball & S. W. Freedman (Eds.), *Bakhtinian perspectives on language, literacy, and learning*. New York, NY: Cambridge University Press.

Beers, K. (2003). *When kids can't read: What teachers can do*. Portsmouth, NH: Heinemann.

Bell, D. (2004). *Silent covenants: Brown v. Board of Education and the unfulfilled hopes for racial reform*. New York, NY: Oxford University Press.

Boaler, J., & Greeno, J. G. (2000). Identity, agency and knowing in mathematics worlds. In J. Boaler (Ed.), *Multiple perspectives on mathematics teaching and learning* (pp. 171–200). Westport, CT: Ablex.

Bowlby, J. (1973). *Attachment and loss, Vol. 2: Separation*. New York, NY: Basic Books.

Bowles, S., & Gintis, H. (1976). *Schooling in capitalist America*. New York, NY: Basic Books.

Boyle, G. (2010). *Tattoos on the heart: The power of boundless compassion*. New York, NY: Free Press.

Brave Heart, M. Y. H., & Deschenie, T. (2006). Resource guide: Historical trauma and post-colonial stress in American Indian populations. *Tribal College Journal of American Indian Education, 17*(3), 24–27.

Brooke, R. (1987). Underlife and writing instruction. *College Composition and Communication, 38*, 141–153.

Bruner, J. S. (1993). The autobiographical process. In R. Folkenflik (Ed.), *The culture of autobiography: Constructions of self-representation*. Stanford, CA: Stanford University Press.

Bruner, J. S. (2004). Life as narrative. *Social Research, 71,* 691–710.

Burke, K. (1953). *Counterstatement.* New York, NY: Harcourt.

Burroughs, A. (2002). *Running with scissors.* New York, NY: Picador.

Burton, C. L., & King, L. A. (2004). The health benefits of writing about intensely positive experiences. *Journal of Research in Personality, 38,* 150–163.

Campbell, R. S., & Pennebaker, J. W. (2003). The secret life of pronouns: Flexibility in writing style and physical health. *Psychological Science, 14*(1), 60-65.

Christenson, S. L., & Havsy, L. H. (2004). Family-school-peer relationships: Significance for social, emotional, and academic learning. In J. E. Zins, R. P. Weissberg, M. C. Wang, & H. J. Walberg (Eds.), *Building academic success on social and emotional learning: What does the research say?* (pp. 59–75). New York, NY: Teachers College Press.

Coles, R. (1989). *The call of stories.* Boston, MA: Houghton Mifflin.

Connor, J. O., & Pope, D. C. (2013). Not just robo-students: Why full engagement matters and how schools can promote it. *Journal of Youth and Adolescence, 42,* 1426–1442.

Conway, M., Singer, J. A., & Tagini, A. (2004). The self and autobiographical memory: Correspondence and coherence. *Social Cognition, 22*(5), 491–529.

Cuban, L. (2004). *The blackboard and the bottom line: Why schools can't be businesses.* Cambridge, MA: Harvard University Press.

Danielewicz, J. (2008). "Personal genres, public voices." *College Composition and Communication, 59*(3), 420–450.

Darling-Hammond, L. (2010). *The flat world and education: How American's commitment to equity will determine our future.* New York, NY: Teachers College Press.

Deci, E. L., Schwartz, A., Sheinman, L., & Ryan, R. M. (1981). An instrument to assess adult's orientations toward control versus autonomy in children: Reflections on intrinsic motivation and perceived competence. *Journal of Educational Psychology, 74,* 642–650.

Degruy, J. (2005). *Post traumatic slave syndrome: America's legacy of enduring injury and healing.* Milwaukie, OR: Uptone Press.

Demorest, A. P., & Alexander, I. E. (1992). Affective scripts as organizers of personal experience. *Journal of Personality, 60,* 645–663.

Denard, C. (Ed.). (2008). *Toni Morrison Conversations.* Jackson: University Press of Mississippi.

Dewey, J. (1900). *The child and the curriculum.* Chicago, IL: University of Chicago Press.

Donley, S., Habib, L., Jovanovic, T., Kamkwalala, A., Evces, M., Egan, G., Bradley, B., & Ressler, K. J. (2012). Civilian PTSD symptoms and risk for involvement in the criminal justice system. *Journal of the American Academy of Psychiatry and the Law, 40,* 522–529.

Dreher E., & Dreher, M. (1991). Developmentally consequential events as viewed by adolescents. *Schweizerische Zeitschrift fur Psychologie, 50,* 24–33.

Dyson, A. H., & Genishi, C. (1994). *The need for story*. Urbana, IL: National Council of Teachers of English.

Elbow, P. (1973). *Writing without teachers*. New York: Oxford University Press.

Elbow, P. (1991). Reflections on academic discourse: How it relates to freshmen and colleagues. *College English, 53*, 135–155.

Elbow, P. (1995). Being a writer vs. being an academic: A conflict in goals. *Composition and Communication, 46*, 72–83.

Elbow, P. (1997). High stakes and low stakes in assigning and responding to writing. In M. D. Sorcinelli & P. Elbow (Eds.), *Writing to learn: Strategies for assigning and responding to writing across the disciplines*. San Francisco, CA: Jossey-Bass.

Elbow, P. (2000). *Everyone can write: Essays toward a hopeful theory of writing and teaching writing*. New York, NY: Oxford University Press.

Elbow, P., & Belanoff, P. (2000). *Sharing and responding*. New York, NY: McGraw-Hill.

Erbentraut, J. (2015, April 29). School may be the best place to address PTSD in young people, but resources are spread thin. *The Huffington Post*.

Erikson, E. H. (1968). *Identity: Youth and crisis*. New York, NY: Norton.

Felitti, V. J., Anda, R. F., & Nordenberg, D., Williamson, D. F., Spitz, A. M., Edwards, V., . . . Marks, J. S. (1998). Relationship of childhood abuse and household dysfunction to many of the leading causes of death in adults. The Adverse Childhood Experiences (ACE) Study. *American Journal of Preventative Medicine, 14*(4), 245–258.

Flores-González, N. (2002). *School kids/street kids: Identity development in Latino students*. New York, NY: Teachers College Press.

Florio-Ruane, S. (1997). To tell a new story: Reinventing narratives of culture, identity, and education. *Anthropology & Education Quarterly, 28*, 152–162.

Fredericks, J. A., Blumenfeld, P. C., & Paris, A. H. (2004). School engagement: Potential of the concept, state of the evidence. *Review of Educational Research, 74*(1), 59–109.

Freire. P. (1987). The importance of the act of reading. In P. Freire & D. Macedo, *Literacy: Reading the word and the world*. Westport, CT: Bergin & Garvey.

Goleman, D. (1995). *Emotional intelligence*. New York, NY: Bantam.

Greenberg, M. T., Cicchetti, D., & Cummings, E. M. (1990). *Attachment in the preschool years: Theory, research and intervention*. Chicago, IL: University of Chicago Press.

Greene, M. (1974). *Landscapes of learning*. New York, NY: Teachers College Press.

Greene, M. (1994). Multiculturalism, community, and the arts. In A. H. Dyson and C. Genishi (Eds.), *The need for story*. Urbana, IL: National Council of Teachers of English.

Guardo, C. J., & Bohan, J. B. (1971). Development of a sense of self-identity in children. *Child Development, 42*, 1909–1921.

Gunderson, J. G. (2009). Borderline personality disorder: Ontogeny of a diagnosis. *American Journal of Psychiatry, 166*, 530–539.

Gutiérrez, K., Rymes, B., & Larson, J. (1995). Script, counterscript, and underlife in the classroom: James Brown versus Brown v. Board of Education. *Harvard Educational Review, 65*(3), 445–471.

Habermas, T., & Bluck, S. (2000). Getting a life: The emergence of the life story in adolescence. *Psychological Bulletin, 126,* 748–769.

Harris, N. B. (2014, September). Nadine Burke Harris: How childhood trauma affects health across a lifetime [Video file]. Retrieved from *https://www.ted.com/talks/ nadine_burke_harris_how_childhood_trauma_affects_health_across_a_lifetime?language=en*

Hartman, G. (1958). Milton's counterplot. *English Literary History, 25*(1). 1–12.

hooks, b. (1994). *Teaching to transgress: Education as the practice of freedom.* New York, NY: Routledge.

hooks, b. (2000). *All about love: New visions.* New York, NY: HarperCollins.

Independent Media Institute. (2015, August). *Why there are high rates of PTSD in this teacher's classroom.* San Francisco, CA: Emily Wilson.

Johnson, D. W. & Johnson, R. T. (2004). The three Cs of promoting social and emotional learning. In J. E. Zins, R. P. Weissberg, M. C. Wang, & H. J. Walberg (Eds.), *Building academic success on social and emotional learning: What does the research say?* (pp. 59–75). New York, NY: Teachers College Press

Klein, D. (1972). Drug therapy as a means of syndrome identification and nosological revision. In J. Cole, A. Freeman, & A. Friedhoff (Eds), *Psychopathy and Psychopharmacology.* Baltimore, MD: Johns Hopkins University Press

Kohl, H. (1991). *I won't learn from you: The role of assent in learning.* Minneapolis, MN: Milkweed Editions.

Kristeva, J. (1980). *Desire in language: A semiotic approach to literature and art.* New York, NY: Columbia University Press.

Ladson-Billings, G. (1995). Toward a theory of culturally relevant pedagogy. *American Educational Research Journal, 32*(3), 465–491.

Ladson-Billings, G. (2001). *Crossing over to Canaan: The journey of new teachers in diverse classrooms.* San Francisco, CA: Jossey-Bass.

Lee, C. D. (1995). A culturally based cognitive apprenticeship: Teaching African American high school students skills in literary interpretation. *Reading Research Quarterly, 30*(4), 608–630.

Lee, C. D. (2007). *Culture, literacy, and learning: Taking bloom in the midst of the whirlwind.* New York, NY: Teachers College Press.

Likona, T. (1991). *Educating for character.* New York, NY: Bantam.

Lunsford, A. (2007). *Writing matters: Rhetoric in public and private lives.* Athens: University of Georgia Press.

Marks, H. (2000). Student engagement in instructional activity: Patterns in the elementary, middle, and high school years. *American Educational Research Journal, 37*(1), 153–184.

Marshall, B. (2012, August 17). *Brandon Marshall's project borderline.* Retrieved from http://projectborderline.org/Official_Site/Home.html

Mayer, J. D., & Salovey, P. (1997), What is emotional intelligence? In P. Salovey & D. J. Slutyer (Eds.), *Emotional development and emotional intelligence.* New York, NY: Basic Books.

McAdams, D.P. (1993). *The stories we live by: Personal myths and the making of the self.* New York, NY: William Morrow.

McAdams, D.P. (1996). Personality, modernity, and the storied self: A contemporary framework for studying persons. *Psychological Inquiry, 7,* 295-321.

McAdams, D. P. (1998). The role of defense in the life story. *Journal of Personality, 66*(4), 1125–1146.

McAdams, D. P., & Bowman, P. J. (2001). Narrating life's turning points: Redemption and contamination. In D. McAdams, R. Josselson, & A Lieblich (Eds.), *Turns in the road: Narrative studies of lives in transition* (pp. 3–34). Washington DC: American Psychological Association.

Milton. J. (2007). Paradise lost. In In W. Kerrigan, J. Rumrich, & S. M. Fallon (Eds.), *The complete poetry and essential prose of John Milton.* New York, NY: Random House.

Miron, G., & Nelson, C. (2002). *What's public about charter schools? Lessons learned about choice and accountability.* Thousand Oaks, CA: Corwin Press.

Mohr, D. M. (1978). Development of attributes of personal identity. *Developmental Psychology, 14,* 427–428.

Morrison, T. (1977). *Song of Solomon.* New York, NY: Vintage.

Morrison, T. (1987). The site of memory. In *Inventing the truth: The art and craft of memoir.* Boston, MA: Houghton Mifflin.

Nasir, N. S., McLaughlin, M. W., & Jones, A. (2009). What does it mean to be African-American? Constructions of race and academic identity in an urban public high school. *American Educational Research Journal, 46*(1), 73-114.

Nasir, N. S., Jones, A., & McLaughlin, M. W. (2011). School connectedness for students in low-income urban high schools. *Teachers College Record, 113*(8), 1755–1793.

Newkirk, T. (1997). *The performance of self in student writing.* Portsmouth, NH: Heinemann.

Newkirk, T. (2014). *Minds made for stories: How we really read and write informational and persuasive texts.* Portsmouth, NH: Heinemann.

Newmann, F. M. (1992). *Student engagement and achievement in American secondary schools.* New York, NY: Teachers College Press.

Noguera, P. A. (2003). Schools, prisons, and social implications of punishment: Rethinking disciplinary practices. *Theory into Practice, 42*(4), 341–350.

Noguera, P. A. (2008). What discipline is for: Connecting students to the benefits of learning. In M. Pollock (Ed.), *Everyday antiracism: Getting real about race in schools* (pp. 132–138). New York, NY: The New Press.

Nussbaum, M. (1995). *Poetic justice: The literary imagination and public life.* Boston, MA: Beacon Press.

Oakes, J. (1985). *Keeping track: How schools structure inequality.* New Haven, CT: Yale University Press.

Oakes, J., & Wells, A. (1998). Detracking for high school achievement. *Educational Leadership, 56*, 38–41.

Odell, L., Goswami, D., & Herrington, A. (1983). The discourse-based interview: A procedure for exploring the tacit knowledge of writers in non-academic settings. In P. Mosenthal, L. Tamor, & S. Walmsley (Eds.), *Research on writing.* (pp. 221236). New York, NY: Longman.

Olick, J. (2008). The ciphered transits of collective memory: Neo-Freudian impressions. *Social Research, 75*(1), 1–22.

Palmer, P. J. (1999). Evoking the spirit in public education. *Educational Leadership, 56*(4), 6–11.

Pennebaker, J. W., & Seagal, J. D. (1999). Forming a story: The health benefits of narrative. *Journal of Clinical Psychology, 55*(10), 1243–1254.

Penuel, W., & Wertsch, J. (1995). Vygotsky and identity formation: A sociocultural approach. *Educational Psychologist, 30*, 83–92.

Perry, B. D., & Szalavitz, M. (2006). *The boy who was raised as a dog: What traumatized children can teach us about loss, love, and healing.* New York, NY: Basic Books.

Peshkin, A. (2000). *The color of strangers, the color of friends.* Chicago, IL: University of Chicago Press.

Piaget, J. (1968). *Six psychological studies.* New York, NY: Random House.

Pope, D. (2001). *Doing school.* New Haven, CT: Yale University Press.

Propublica. (2014, February). *The PTSD crisis that's being ignored: Americans wounded in their own neighborhoods.* New York, NY: Lois Beckett.

Reeve, J., Jang, H., Carrell, D., Jeon, S., & Barch, J. (2004). Enhancing students' engagement by increasing teachers' autonomy support. *Motivation and Emotion, 28*, 147–169.

Reveles, J. M., & Brown, B. A. (2008). Contextual shifting: Teachers emphasizing students' academic identity to promote scientific literacy. *Science Education, 92*(6), 1015–1041.

Reveles, J. M., Cordova, R., & Kelly, G. J. (2004). Science literacy and academic identity formation. *Journal of Research in Science Teaching, 41*(10), 1111–1144.

Rich, A. (1979). *On lies, secrets, and silence: Selected prose 1966–1978.* New York, NY: Norton.

Rios, V. (2011). *Punished: Policing the lives of Black and Latino boys.* New York: New York University Press.

Rodriguez, L. (2001). *Hearts and hands: Creating community in violent times.* New York, NY: Seven Stories Press

Rose, M. (1989). *Lives on the boundary: A moving account of the struggles and achievements of America's educationally underprepared.* New York, NY: Penguin.

Salovey, P., & Mayer, J. D. (1990). Emotional intelligence. *Imagination, Cognition, & Personality, 9*, 185–211.

Schacter, D. L. (2001). *The seven sins of memory.* New York, NY: Houghton Mifflin.

Schoenbach, R., Greenleaf, C., & Murphy, L. (2012). *Reading for understanding.* San Francisco, CA: Jossey-Bass.

Scholes, R. (1985). *Textual power: Literary theory and the teaching of English.* New Haven, CT: Yale University Press.

Schultz, W.T. (2001). De profundis: Prison as a turning point in Oscar Wilde's life story. In D. McAdams, R. Josselson, & A Lieblich (Eds.), *Turns in the road: Narrative studies of lives in transition* (pp. 67–90). Washington DC: American Psychological Association.

Shernoff, D. J., Csikszentmihalyi, M., Schneider, B., & Shernoff, E. S. (2003). Student engagement in high school classrooms from the perspective of flow theory. *School Psychology Quarterly, 18*(2), 158–176.

Shor, I. (1987). *Freire for the classroom: A sourcebook for liberatory teaching.* Portsmouth, NH: Heinemann.

Shor, I., & Freire, P. (1987). *A pedagogy for liberation: Dialogues on transforming education.* Westport, CT: Bergin & Garvey Publishers, Inc.

Shulman, L. (1986). Those who understand: Knowledge growth in teaching. *Educational Researcher, 15*(2), 4–14.

Singer, J. A. (2001). Living in the amber cloud: A life story analysis of a heroine addict. In D. McAdams, R. Josselson, & A Lieblich (Eds.), *Turns in the road: Narrative studies of lives in transition* (pp. 253–277). Washington DC: American Psychological Association.

Singer, J. A. (2005). *Memories that matter.* Oakland, CA: New Harbinger.

Sleeter, C. (2001). Preparing teachers for culturally diverse schools: Research and the overwhelming presence of whiteness. *Journal of Teacher Education, 52*(2), 94–106.

Spence, D. P. (1982). Narrative truth and theoretical truth. *Psychoanalytic Quarterly, 51*(1), 43–69.

Steele, C. (1997). A threat in the air: How stereotypes shape intellectual identity and performance. *American Psychologist, 52*(6), 613–639.

Stock, P. (1995). *The dialogic curriculum: Teaching and learning in a multicultural society.* Portsmouth, NH: Heinemann.

Sullivan, P. (2003). Composing culture: A place for the personal. *College English, 66,* 41–54.

Szalavitz, M., & Perry, B. D. (2014). *Born for love.* New York, NY: HarperCollins.

Taylor-Guthrie, D. (Ed.). (1994). *Conversations with Toni Morrison.* Jackson: University Press of Mississippi.

Tomkins, S. (1987). Script theory. In J. Aranoff, A. I. Rabin, & R. A. Zucker (Eds.), *The emergence of personality* (pp. 147–216). New York, NY: Springer.

Valencia, R. R. (2005). The Mexican American struggle for equal educational opportunity in Mendez v. Westminster: Helping to pave the way for Brown v. Board of Education. *Teachers College Record, 107*(3), 389–423.

Van Gelder, K. (2010). *The Buddha and the borderline: My recovery from borderline personality disorder through dialectical behavior therapy, Buddhism, and online dating.* Oakland, CA: New Harbinger.

Varenne, H., & McDermott, R. (1999). *Successful failure: The school America builds*. Boulder, CO: Westview Press.

Vygotsky, L. S. (1978). *Mind and society*. Cambridge, MA: Harvard University Press.

Wells, A. S. (2002). *Where charter school policy fails: The problems of accountability and equity*. New York, NY: Teachers College Press.

Wertsch, J. (2008). Collective memory and memory templates. *Social Research*, 75(1), 133–155.

Wischnia, S., Nasir, N., LaMay, B., O'Connor, K., & Sullivan, S. (May, 2010). It's in the meaning: Refining the concept of academic identity. Presented at the annual meeting of the American Educational Research Association, Denver, CO.

Yale, K (Producer). (2015). *The battle for public education in the 21st century* [Radio Program]. Berkeley, CA: Pacifica Radio.

Yazzie-Mintz, E. (2007). *Voices of students on engagement: A report on the 2006 high school survey of student engagement*. Bloomington, IN: Center for Evaluation and Educational Policy.

Yazzie-Mintz, E., & McCormick, K. (2012). Finding the humanity in the data: Understanding, measuring, and strengthening student engagement. In S. L. Christenson, A. Reschly, & C. Wiley (Eds), *Handbook of research on student engagement* (pp. 743–761). New York, NY: Springer.

Zehr, H. (2002). *The little book of restorative justice*. Intercourse, PA: Good Books.

Zins, J. E., & Elias, M. J. (2006). Social-emotional learning: Promoting the development of all students. *Journal of Educational and Psychological Consultation*, 17(2&3), 233–255.

# Index

References for figures are followed by the letter *f*.

# About the Author

***Bronwyn Clare LaMay*** is currently a high school English teacher and coach in Hayward, California. Prior to this, she was a teacher and administrator in Oakland. She began her career in a public middle school and has since taught middle and high school in multiple Bay area cities. She has also worked as a master teacher for KQED in San Francisco and taught community college courses in the state penal system. In addition to her K-12 work, she has lectured in schools of education at Mills College, Stanford University, UC Santa Cruz, and UC Berkeley. Bronwyn currently lives in Oakland.